U0139387

四幕舞台劇

姜龍昭 著

蔣 娉 譯

李商隱之戀

文史哲出版社印行

國立中央圖書館出版品預行編目資料

李商隱之戀：四幕舞台劇 = The Poet's Story
: an original play / 姜龍昭；蔣娉譯. --
初版. -- 臺北市：文史哲，民84
　　面；公分
ISBN 957-547-983-1(平裝)

854.6

李商隱之戀

著　者：姜　　　龍　　　昭
出版者：文　史　哲　出　版　社
登記證字號：行政院新聞局局版臺業字五三三七號
發行人：彭　　　正　　　雄
發行所：文　史　哲　出　版　社
印刷者：文　史　哲　出　版　社
台北市羅斯福路一段七十二巷四號
郵撥〇五一二八八一二彭正雄帳戶
電話：三　五　一　一　〇　二　八

中華民國八十四年十二月初版

實價新台幣二八〇元

這是我從事寫作五十年，出版的第五十二本著作，也是我編寫舞台劇本中，第四本有中英文翻譯對照的劇本。歡迎大家批評、指教，並演出。

姜龍昭 識

八十四年十月臺北

饒　序

龍昭兄又要出版劇本了，他特地跑來看我，和我談起他編寫「李商隱之戀」的經過，滿臉意興飛揚。三十年來，他專注投入劇本的創作，鍥而不捨，雖已從「中視」退休，但在退休之後，並未悠遊林下，輕鬆度日，反而更是全力以赴的寫作和研究，自己在家中成立「編劇研究班」，似乎比從前上班還忙碌，他的精神，的確令人佩服。

我和龍昭，民國五十一年同一時期進入電視台工作，那時真的年少樂觀，我們對電影戲劇，都同樣有著一股熱情，我在報紙和雜誌都闢有影評專欄，常要看電影和寫影評，而龍昭的記性特好，常能對老片子和老明星，大談其從影的來龍去脈，興緻昂然，彼此常談得非常開心，那時他已不斷的寫劇本，電視劇和廣播劇是他常寫的，但最為陶醉的還是舞台劇本，不多時他就會寫出一本，是個多產作家，取材的範圍相當廣泛，幾乎什麼都寫，再加上他又相當熱心和活躍，他在文壇上很快成了一個「熱門人物」。

這本「李商隱之戀」是他花了很多心思的結晶，而且做了很多考證工夫，龍昭對於歷史人物的考

證，曾著迷一個時期，他對「香妃」的用功和用心，曾使很多歷史學家為之刮目相看，大為讚賞，「李商隱之戀」應是繼「香妃」考證之後，着力甚深的劇作，其間數度修改，數度增刪，編寫態度嚴謹認真，他描述詩人李商隱這一段纏綿而無奈的感情，落筆細膩而生動，讀來甚為感人。

李商隱是晚唐詩人，他的詩充滿了浪漫情調，讓人喜悅，讓人迷思，和李杜的詩作，風格大為不同，龍昭就李商隱的浪漫才情和愛情遭遇，用來構成戲劇素材，使觀眾可以由舞台的演出，而窺知李商隱內心的感性世界，進而了解晚唐時代的社會生態，以及其對於當時個人所處地位的影響力量，這也是造成本劇內在與外在衝突的重要因素。

本劇已完成英譯工作，是由昔為著名演員現為英譯名家蔣娉小姐擔任，歷史劇英譯，這是相當吃重的翻譯，好在蔣娉女士的文學底子深厚，且一心一意要把李商隱介紹給英美人士，這是很有意義的事，我們最希望的，還是「李商隱之戀」早些在舞台上演現，不僅在國內，同時也在國外。

饒曉明（魯稚子）一九九五年八月初臺北炎夏

黃　序

晚唐詩人中，李商隱的詩，善於用典，沈博絕麗，在解與不解之間，千年以來，不知風靡了多少詩迷。回憶十年前在「中央副刊」時，曾與夏鐵肩兄談及「錦瑟無端五十弦」一詩，誰知鐵肩兄更是義山迷，在青年時期便能背誦整集，集句成章，可以信手拈來，天衣無縫；與他暢談玉谿生的詩，是那時我最快樂的一段時光。

李義山詩宗老杜，博極羣書，無一語，無來歷，加之他思路深奧，下筆馨殫精神，又窮極精巧，是以他的詩最稱難懂，千年以來，不知迷惑了多少人。到他逝後四百年，連七歲能詩，淹博經傳百家的元遺山（一一九○～一二五七年），也都認為義山詩沒有注本是一大恨事：「望帝春心託杜鵑，佳人錦瑟怨華年，詩家總愛西崑好，只恨無人作鄭箋。」

詩如其人，李義山一生既愛國，有些詩如漢宮、瑤池，「指事懷忠，鬱紆激切」，可是他一生並不得志，玉台、香奩諸詩，一半寫的是閨闈綺情，偏偏是這些詩，受人喜愛却隱晦難解。使人聯想，他一生究竟如何？姜龍昭兄的大著「李商隱之戀」，便為我們作了解答。

龍昭兄為戲劇大家，復擅考據，他寫這個劇本，態度極為慎重，不但讀遍義山詩文，還遍及十餘

家的箋註，請教各名家「鄭箋無人」的憾事，終於在他推求至隱解恨有道下，使讀者能直窺這位大詩

人坎坷一生中的脆弱心靈。歷史上自創以對話的方式，使這位大詩人活生生呈現在現代觀眾、聽眾、

與讀者前。一千兩百年後，有龍昭兄的慧眼靈心和如椽巨筆巧為剖析，義山有此知己，可以無憾了。

不過，龍昭兄說義山得年四十七歲，與我所知似略有出入，以對義山生卒年的考證來說，馮浩所

編的年譜，說他生於唐德宗貞元十五年（七九九年），卒於懿宗咸通二年（八六一年），年六十二歲，兩

夢星則以為生於唐憲宗元和八年（八一三年），卒於宣宗大中八年（八五四年），得年四十一歲。程

說相差達二十一歲。朱注則為義山訂詩譜著手，認為他當生於貞元十二年間（七九五～七九六年），卒

於大中咸通之間（八五九～八六○年），大約六十來歲，依義山詩文所述推斷，這是較為落實的一種

推算。（龍昭註）

不過，劇本不同於傳記或者小說，年歲的差異，並不會有重大的影響。

龍昭兄其所以編成舞台劇本，求其可以垂諸久遠，然而，一旦經過高手譯為外文，李商隱的故事

就更能遍及海角天涯，使外國讀者，也能沉浸在這位「中國拜倫」一生，「遙情婉變，纏綿宕往」的

詩心中了。

蔣娉女士前曾譯過龍昭兄「淚水的沉思」、「飛機失事以後」與「泣血煙花」三個劇本，本劇更

忠實於原著，而流暢於對白，可以不經潤色，立即可以上演，見地獨到，譯筆也獨得流暢自如之美，

讀來一泓水暢，實則她沉浸兩種語文甚深，往返出入，看似了無滯礙，定下過許多苦工夫。我對她這次譯的

龍昭兒以前的三個劇本，對人名的迻譯，深得我心，能使西洋讀者沉浸其中，無所隔閡。但這次譯的

歷史劇，確有其人其事，不免在譯名的第一關，就受到了約束，使人擊節的是，她譯此劇劇中人的名

字，採取霍克斯譯「紅樓夢」的雙重路線：主角譯音，而次角譯義。如寶玉譯Bao-yu，元春譯Yuan

-chun，警幻仙姑則譯Disenchantment，香憐和玉愛譯Darling和Preciaus，劉姥姥則半音半義，

譯為Grannie Liu。譯名方式不從一而終，在說部長篇中，才能維持讀者的注意力。

蔣譯「李商隱之戀」也採用霍式譯法，主角李商隱譯Lee，韓畏之譯Han，商隱的小弟慶宇，不

譯姓而逕譯Ching-yu，以免造成混淆，令狐絢爲雙姓，也只簡譯爲Nien：而女主角盧輕鳳譯爲「鳳

凰」Phoenix，貼身宮女彩玉譯Jade，小黃門來喜則譯Merry，都譯爲貼切可喜。只不過譯盧飛鸞的

英文名，以一句流行話來說，叫Argus，似大沉重，很多人可能只會想到希臘神話中的百眼巨人阿耳

戈斯，不太會想到這是「大雄」或者「鸞雞」Argus pheasant。不過英文的確沒有與「鸞」相對應

的字兒。譯人遇到這種冷僻名字，也都難免有無力感。

關於「李」的英譯，Lee或Li均可，我國總統、副總統都姓李，但英文譯法各異，總統李登輝爲

Lee Tung-hui，副總統李元簇却是Li Yuan-zu。不過李商隱已有譯名Li Shang-yin，如採舊譯，

西方讀者就不會鬧雙包案了。

黃文範　中華民國八十四年八月十日

龍昭註：

關於李商隱之生卒年月，過去確有多種不同的說法，盛如黃文範先生在序文中說，有說他活了四十一歲，有說他活了六十二歲，也有說大約六十來歲。

據我所查的資料。明朝研究玉谿生詩箋者，有錢龍惕。

清朝研究李義山詩箋者，計有：朱鶴齡、吳喬、陸崑曾、姚培謙、屈復、程夢星、馮浩、沈厚塽、紀昀等人，其中，以馮浩、程夢星、朱鶴齡較為深入精闢。而為李商隱編「年譜」者，首創於朱鶴齡。然亦僅稍具規模，致產生多種不同之說法。

民國以來，研究李商隱者，計有張采田、顧翊群、汪辟疆、徐復觀、吳調公、蘇雪林、朱偰、藍于、楊柳、劉維崇、董乃斌、董明鈞、傅錫壬等人，均有專著發表。

其中，錢塘張采田先生，復集古人今人之大成，取朱鶴齡以下，諸人考訂之年譜，細加整理，訂其偽，增其闕，修其繁，完成「玉谿生年譜會箋」四卷。（劉氏求恕齋叢書）本劇所確定李商隱生卒年月，即依張氏修訂之年譜，特說明之。

自 序

一、

民國卅四年，抗戰勝利的那年，我在故鄉蘇州，開始投稿寫作，迄民國八十四年，屈指算來，已五十週年了。

在這漫長的五十年中，我已出版了五十一本書，獲得了四十六項不同的獎，可謂收穫不少。

最先我寫小品、散文、方塊、小說，以後又寫新詩。卅八年開始嘗試寫劇本，先是舞台劇，接着是廣播劇、電視劇，最後是電影劇本。陸陸續續各種劇本，都出版過單行本。

最近這十年，我開始喜歡寫傳記文學、歷史考證、以及歷史舞台劇。

因着閱讀蘇雪林教授的「玉溪詩謎正續合編」這本書，使我興起了編寫「李商隱之戀」舞台劇本的念頭，因為過去從未有人寫過有關李商隱的劇本。

從消化歷史資料到完成初稿，前後歷時三年，再經過不斷的請人過目，修訂，前後六易其稿，至最後定稿，已歷時五年。閱讀參考書籍廿八種，書目另詳。

該劇初稿完成後，曾於民國八十一年獲教育部文藝創作舞台劇本類優勝獎，以後改為廣播劇，分上、下兩集，在中廣公司播出後，又獲中華民國編劇學會頒給最佳廣播劇編劇「魁星獎」。得了兩項獎，我仍覺不滿意，為求完美，我又多方蒐集晚唐史料，將第一幕澈底重寫，另增加了「序幕」及「尾聲」，才算定稿，這在我四十多年的編劇生涯中，是絕無僅有的，特在此說明，詳細之寫作經過，可參閱「我寫李商隱之戀劇本經過」一文，此處不再贅述。

二、

為求使本劇傳諸後世，推展至海外國際舞台演出，我特請已翻譯過我三本舞台劇本：「淚水的沉思」、「飛機失事以後」、「泣血煙花」的翻譯高手蔣娉女士，將之譯成英文，好中英對照，一併出版。

過去三本劇本，均是現代時裝劇，比較好譯，這本「李商隱之戀」是歷史人物劇，且劇中穿插了不少李商隱傳誦千古的「名詩」，要將之譯成英文，困難度提高了很多，但蔣女士勇敢的接受了此項挑戰，經過了幾近一年的推敲，始譯畢全劇，包括我第五次的修改本，在翻譯期間，她又仔細的挑出一些她認為不妥的地方，讓我作了第六次的修訂。

她確定本劇的英文劇名為：「The Poet's Story」她認為「詩人的故事」較為高雅，不必強調愛情，因劇中尚有李商隱的宦海浮沉及性格描述，美國許多介紹藝術家、音樂家的愛情故事，在片名

上，也皆不用「愛」字，李商隱是晚唐的名詩人，有其特殊的地位，不必過分強調其名字，避免一般讀者，因不諳其名而退却觀賞。

其次，劇中人名，大部份用音譯或者以名稱、職位而定。女主角「輕鳳」及「飛鸞」，則用意譯，以呈現她倆優美的形象。翻譯「紅樓夢」的名家，也都半採用此種雙重譯法，詳見翻譯名家黃文範先生所寫之序文。

至於李商隱之詩作，中詩英譯，各界不儘相同，很難一致，蔣娉女士一方面摘錄了Wilter Bynner的譯句，一方面自己也翻譯了一遍，同時陳現，供讀者自由選擇，Wilter Bynner不知現居何處，無法與之取得聯絡，若他看到，亦希他能同意及諒解。

蔣娉女士，為譯本劇，她用心而又敬業，確實化了相當的精神與心血，在現今的社會中，殊為不易。

為了讓大家，對蔣娉女士，多一點認識，我這裡簡單的，向大家作一番介紹。

她是中國人，祖籍江西九江，四川隆昌出生，在臺灣臺北長大，於一九六一年（民國五十年），在臺灣加入中央電影公司為基本演員，與影星王莫愁、丁強等合作拍攝過電影「蚵女」一片，及後又演出過劉碩夫導演的舞台劇：「旋風」。民國五十一年十月，臺灣電視公司開播，五十二年她與林機、方靜靜、王戎合作在臺視演出「青春三鳳」劇集、與巴戈演出「溫暖人間」等電視劇，另外還擔任過電視節目「黃金時代」的主持人工作。

一九六四年她考入民航空運公司出任ＣＡＴ空中小姐，一九六八年進入美國紐約派克學院（

Packer Collgiate Institne）研究文學與戲劇，此一期間，她用心研讀了不少世界聞名的舞台劇本。

一九七〇年進入美國紐澤西州瑞格士大學道格拉斯女子學院（Douglass College Rntgers

University American Studies. B. A）繼續深造，主修美國文化研究，獲文學士學位。

迄一九九五年，前後在美居留了廿八年之久，因她的夫婿是美國人，所以她對中文，英文均有相

當的造詣，本劇譯畢後，並特請她夫婿John Sawyer Moxon予以細加校正，以求慎重。

我與蔣娉女士，相識於民國五十二年，那時我在臺灣電視公司任編審，並兼任「青春三鳳」節目

製作人。五十三年，她去了美國，就再也沒有聯絡，想不到民國七十九年，她回到臺北，才再度相見，相

隔了廿多年，她對戲劇的狂熱，依舊不減當年，當民國八十年十月，臺北的「眞善美劇團」演出我編

寫的「一隻古瓶」舞台劇時，她竟不計待遇，自費搭機專程返國，特來參予該劇之演出。八十年開始

着手英譯我的舞台劇本。

八十四年七月，她的小女兒莫瓏珊，來臺北劍潭參加救國團舉辦的「海外青年學習中心」研習中

文，可見她雖人在美國，仍熱愛中國，教導她的子女，不忘學習中文。

我為了愼重起見，將蔣娉的譯稿付印前，特寄請此間的翻譯名家黃文範先生賜教，若有不妥之處，希

他提出，以便改正。

蒙黃文範先生厚愛，百忙中為本劇之中英文部份，作了一次詳細的檢查。中文部份，他對李商隱

的生卒年月，提出了不同的說法，對我在劇中，肯定他活了四十七歲，表示存疑。為此，我又翻查了

手邊的多種書籍，特加註說明如下：

據我所查的資料。明朝研究「玉谿生詩箋」者，有錢龍惕。

清朝研究「李義山詩箋」者，計有：朱鶴齡、吳喬、陸崑曾、姚培謙、屈復、程夢星、馮浩、沈

厚塽、紀昀等人，其中，以馮浩、程夢星、朱鶴齡較為深入精闢。而為李商隱編「年譜」者，首創於

朱鶴齡。然亦僅稍具規模，致產生不同之說法。

民國以來，研究李商隱者，計有張采田、顧翊群、汪辟疆、徐復觀、吳調公、蘇雪林、朱偰、藍

于、楊柳、劉維崇、董乃斌、董明鈞、傅錫壬等人，均有專著發表。

其中，錢塘張采田先生，復集古人今人之大成，取朱鶴齡以下，諸人考訂之年譜，細加整理，訂

其偽，增其闕，修其繁，完成「玉谿生年譜會箋」四卷。（劉氏求恕齋叢書）本劇所確定李商隱生卒

年月，即依張采田修訂之年譜。

譯文部份，黃先生認為蔣譯流暢自如，了無滯礙。人名英譯，探霍克斯雙重譯法，也貼切可喜。

唯對「李」之英譯，有人譯成Lee，有人譯成Li，而李商隱過去有人譯為Li Shang-yin，今蔣娉

譯為Lee Shang-yni，恐引起洋人產生Lee「雙包」之誤解。我思之良久，好在兩者發音相同，舞台演出，

不會使人聽錯，也就尊重譯者之看法，不再更改了。

黃文範先生所撰之序文，述之甚詳，此處不再重複。

三、

「李商隱之戀」中英文均定稿後，我又請名影評人魯稚子賜序，他也就是中國電視公司現任的副總經理饒曉明先生，也是中國文藝協會及中華民國編劇學會的理事長，卅多年前，我倆同時進入電視界服務，如今我已退休，他仍在電視界工作，身兼多項要職，終日忙碌不休，蒙他不棄，仔細讀畢全劇後，親撰序文，使本劇之出版，益增光彩。

本劇之封面，採用唯一流傳後世之「李商隱畫像」，配以古典圖案，係由中國電視公司美術組組長邱則明先生與名美術設計師楊紀廸小姐共同精心設計，容我在此，向他倆致最高的謝意。

最後，我衷心盼望，本劇能有機會，在國內外的舞台上，早日以中文或英文演出，唯希望劇宜演出前，能尊重著作權，先函臺灣臺北市（一○五）八德路三段十二巷五十七弄十九號四樓，或電話：（○二）五七八五八二○號，徵求本人之同意許可。演出時，更希望註明編劇及譯者姓名，勿任意改動對白及情節，若公開售票作營業性之演出，盼能酌付作者演出版權費，若有意改編爲電影、電視劇，要事先徵求作者之同意。

姜龍昭 寫於民國八十四年八月十六日

二二

「李商隱之戀」 目錄

「李商隱之戀」　四幕舞台劇

我寫「李商隱之戀」劇本經過

姜龍昭

李商隱，字義山，又號玉谿生，是晚唐一位極出色的大詩人。他的詩沈博絕麗，獨闢蹊徑，淒美婉約，雋永清新，千餘年來，受人喜愛，歷久彌新。

他一生坎坷，經歷晚唐朋黨之爭的傾軋，可謂受盡在夾縫中求生存的折磨。在愛情方面，卻多采多姿，但又似隱藏一些難言的苦衷。他留下的「艷情詩」、「無題詩」，綺麗而淒美，婉約而不膚淺，唯辭意隱晦不明，令人困於索解，難以猜透。

國內治李義山詩文者，不下十餘家，其詩箋註，清時有馮浩箋玉谿生詩，樊南文集詳註，錢振倫、錢振常註、樊南文集補編。近有朱鶴齡註李義山詩集、朱偰李商隱詩詮，在大陸有吳調公者，研究李義山達五十年之久，完成了「李商隱研究」一書，尤爲精闢。

唯最難得的是蘇雪林教授。她在民國十六年，於蘇州東吳大學執教時，授課之餘，因深入研究李商隱的詩，先發表了一篇論文，繼而她自述在查證古籍中有如發現了一塊「鑛苗」，經一再鑽研挖掘開鑿，是年出版了一本「玉谿詩謎」，把李義山生前一些隱僻晦澀的詩謎，找出了明確的解答。

原來年輕時候的李商隱，曾先愛上過一個名宋華陽的女道士，後來，竟然與深宮中皇上的一對姊妹花宮嬪，有所接觸，陷入感情的深淵，難以自拔。

在當時的封建時代，這種愛情，一旦曝了光，不但自己的腦袋要搬家，甚至可以連累整個家族，他當然要盡量保守這份秘密，但身為詩人的他，又無法克制自己不用詩來宣洩心靈深處的真情，故乃有一些「無題詩」，留傳於後世。

這份奧秘，只有細心研究的文學家，才能探索找到鑰匙，開鎖進入堂奧。蘇雪林教授一甲子前出版的「玉溪詩謎」問世後，首蒙當時文學家曾孟樸先生（筆名東亞病夫）的讚譽，接著在學術界也跟著引起廣泛的論辯。卅年後，不少學者撰寫了不少論文發表，也有結集出版單行本者。有人頗表贊同蘇說，有人則表示反對，認為不可能發生這樣的戀情。

這引起了蘇雪林教授繼續探尋考證的興趣。又經過了漫長的卅年，她又陸續找到不少新的佐證，使她對玉溪詩謎的解答，有了更為紮實的精闢說明，民國七十五年，她在商務印書館又出版了一本「玉溪詩謎續篇」，內容較正篇益為豐富。

不久，「玉溪詩謎正續合編」出了合訂本。前後歷時一甲子之久，這種情形，在出版界而言，可謂是一「異數」；在學術界來說，更可算得上是一「奇蹟」了。

我與內子柯玉雪，因著研讀這一本「玉溪詩謎正續合編」，觸發了編寫「李商隱」舞臺劇本的想法。因為，許多歷史人物，都有人編寫過舞臺劇本，而「李商隱」卻從無有人寫過。民國五十七年，

商務印書館曾出版過我的電視劇版選集：「碧海青天夜夜心」，但僅是取李商隱的詩句，作為書名而已。有了這樣的念頭，從民國七十九年開始，先研讀蘇著，勾勒出劇中應出場人物，再參閱其他有關李商隱的各種書籍，對他的身世、家庭背景、詩文作品、交往友朋，以及時代動脈作通盤之瞭解，最後依據其年譜，決定劇中的取材範圍。

為求符合史實，不草率著筆，乃與內子柯玉雪專程搭車南下，赴台南蘇雪林教授寓所登門聆教。蘇教授雖已九十餘高齡，耳朵有些重聽，但我用筆在紙上寫明造訪來意後，她一聞提起李商隱來，立刻神采飛揚，滔滔不絕，為我倆敘述她當年考證之經過，並勉勵有加，希望早日樂觀其成。

在她的熱情支持及剴切相助下，我與玉雪合作，先完成了李商隱的廣播劇本，取名：「錦瑟恨史」，於八十年十二月一日，在漢聲廣播電臺「千古風流人物」系列廣播劇中播出，八十一年六月，該廣播劇並由「文史哲出版社」出版了單行本。

廣播劇的長度為五十分鐘，而舞臺劇的長度，至少為二小時，加上舞臺劇又有場景的限制，原想把李商隱一生中，他深愛的三個女人：宋華陽、盧輕鳳、妻子（王茂元之次女）王氏，均納入劇中，但左思右想，幅度過長，困難重重，最後，只好化繁為簡，集中在輕鳳一人身上。

為了配合劇中，有一段道士作法唸經趕鬼的情節，我又參閱了「道壇作法」「道門子弟早晚誦課」等書籍，更專程走訪了三教養聖堂的郭慶瑞導師，荷蒙他熱心教導，受益良多。

經過好幾個月的案頭作業，於八十一年十一月，終於完成了本劇的初稿。惟恐臺詞、結構、情節

諸方面，有所舛誤，特複印多份恭請蘇雪林教授、王方曙教授、王紹清教授，以及戲劇界吳若先生、

鍾雷先生、賈亦棣先生、貢敏先生等過目，賜予教正。

通過諸先進的細心核閱，果眞挑出了不少缺點與疏誤之處，有的逐字逐句，細加推敲，有的提出

原則性的修改意見，我一一虛心接受，其中第一、五兩幕，還重新刪節改寫。脫稿後，參加教育部八

十一年文藝創作獎舞臺劇本類之應徵，倖獲入選，成爲我歷年參加教育部應徵劇本，繼「金蘋果」、

「國魂」、「母親的淚」、「淚水的沉思」後第五部得獎劇本。

得獎後，因未有戲劇團體，演出這個劇本，我乃又細心的將之改編成上、下兩集的「廣播劇」，

於八十二年六月十二日、十九日，分兩次，在中廣第二調頻網播出。臆想不到同年十二月，該劇獲中

華民國編劇學會投票表決，通過頒給最佳廣播劇編劇「魁星獎」。爲此，我還專誠又驅車南下，將錄

音帶播給體弱重聽的蘇雪林教授聆聽，她仔細收聽後表示，無瑕可擊。

但我自己，對舞台劇本第一幕，雖修改多次，仍不覺滿意，因有人認爲戲的衝擊力不夠強，也有

人建議我不妨加寫「序幕」及「尾聲」，以加強全劇詩的氣氛，爲了改寫第一幕，我不斷進出中央圖

書館，及各大書店搜集有關唐史上「甘露之變」的素材，經過了一年多的努力，終於八十四年三月間，完

成了第四次的修訂稿，讓我鬆了一口氣。

在這一年多時間中，我看了高陽先生寫的「鳳尾香羅」小說，我覺得他的取材，缺乏考證依據，

又看了香港能仁學院文史研究碩士白冠雲女士所寫的「李商隱艷情詩之謎」的專著，她完全肯定了蘇

一八

雪林教授的看法。

白冠雲女士的這本專著，曾經香港大學黃康顯博士、陳英豪博士審查通過，並蒙此間國立中山大學張仁青博士推荐而出版，張仁青博士是公認研究李商隱詩作的權威學者，而白女士撰寫此書參攷之書目，包括香港，台灣，大陸三地各書局及雜誌報刊所發表有關李商隱之論著，達五十一種之多，真可謂洋洋大觀。

為求瞭解舞台劇演出時，鼓瑟之情景，我又特地走訪台北能彈古瑟的專家魏德棟教授，蒙他不厭其詳告知我有關「錦瑟」與「瑟」之種種學問，他告訴我瑟這一種彈弦樂器，歷史久遠；要稱「鼓瑟」不能稱「彈瑟」。「儀禮」記載，戰國至秦漢之際，盛行「竽瑟之樂」，魏晉南北朝時期，瑟是伴奏相和歌的常用樂器，隋唐時期用于清樂，以后只用于宮廷雅樂和丁香音樂。目前，在台灣會彈古箏者較多，能「鼓瑟」者找不出幾人，唯魏教授向我表示，來日，若有團體有意演出此劇，他可以提供此項樂器，並願指導七種不同的演奏方法。

我也曾請作曲家，希為李商隱「錦瑟」這首詩譜上樂曲，以便演出時，可以演唱，但一些作曲家，皆忙于作流行歌曲，使我未能如願，頗為遺憾。

蘇雪林教授為考證李商隱的戀愛事蹟，前後歷經了六十年一甲子之久，回顧我卅四年開始寫作迄今，前後也已屆滿五十年，五十年中，雖出版了不少：電影劇本、廣播劇本、電視劇本、小說、評論、考據文字，但近年來，我最偏愛的，仍是舞臺劇本，因其可以經得起時間的考驗，一經出版成書，不僅

三、五年內，可以演出，十年、廿年後，仍有演出的可能。莎士比亞的不朽，因至今仍有人演出他的舞臺劇本，不像廣播劇、電視劇、電影，播演完了，就消失了蹤影。

李商隱是中國晚唐傑出詩人，他生前這一段鮮爲人知的戀愛悲劇，我深盼靠著蘇雪林教授的考證，以及本劇的英譯出版演出，能傳諸後世，爲人所熟知，俾與民間傳說的「梁山伯與祝英臺」相互媲美，永垂不朽。

本劇劇情概要

李商隱，字義山，又號玉谿生，是懷州河內人，出生於唐憲宗元和八年，死於唐宣宗大中十二年，享年僅四十七歲。

他是晚唐最極出的大詩人，他的詩，淒美婉曲，千餘年來，受人喜愛，歷久不衰。他一生坎坷，經歷朋黨之爭的傾軋，可謂受盡折磨，但愛情方面，也遇到不少難言的痛苦，他留下的艷情詩、無題詩，綺艷而不輕薄、婉麗而不膚淺，又有不少的神秘的暗示，令人費解，難以猜透。文學家蘇雪林女士窮畢生之力，深入鑽研考證，終於明白究竟，原來他在年青未婚以前，曾與皇宮中的一個宮嬪名叫盧輕鳳者，有一段刻骨銘心的痛苦戀情，本劇的故事，依照蘇教授之考證：就二人相識相愛之經過，及最後因宮闈內的爭風吃醋，而變成了哀怨纏綿的悲劇，……使詩人為之終身飲恨。

「錦瑟無端五十弦，一弦一柱思華年；莊生曉夢迷蝴蝶，望帝春心託杜鵑；滄海月明珠有淚，藍田日暖玉生煙；此情可待成追憶，只是當時已惘然。」李商隱晚年的這道「錦瑟」詩，不僅當時首屈一指，時至今日，古今詩人中，能寫得如此傳神的，也很少見。

二二

「李商隱之戀」　四幕舞台劇

二二

「李商隱之戀」舞台劇劇本

時間：唐文宗太和九年至唐宣宗大中十二年（公元八三五—八五八）

序　幕—唐宣宗大中十二年冬。（公元八五八）

第一幕—唐文宗太和九年冬。（公元八三五）

第二幕—距第一幕十天後。（公元八三五）

第三幕—唐開成二年（公元八三七）春至夏

第四幕—唐開成四年冬（公元八三九）

尾　聲—唐宣宗大中十二年（公元八五八）

地點：鄭州、長安、曲江

佈景：可全部採用抽象方式設計，亦可用寫實方式設計。

一、序幕、第一幕與尾聲：李商隱家，採竹籬茅舍佈置。舞台正中是大門，進門後是院子，種植有樹木。序幕尾聲均下雪，樹為枯枝有積雪更佳，舞台上是堂屋，舞台兩邊通內室，李

「李商隱之戀」舞台劇劇本

人物：李商隱——字義山，是晚唐傑出之詩人，本劇第一至四幕，他方青春年少，廿四歲至廿八歲之間，談戀愛時，神采煥發，序幕、尾聲時，他已四十七歲，有鬍子，憔悴蒼老，當年即病逝。

韓畏之——字瞻，是李商隱的同科進士，年齡相若，相交甚深，唯仕途順利，家庭幸福，序幕尾聲出場，已四十餘歲，留有鬍子，精神飽滿，與商隱成強烈對比。與商隱是連襟。

李　母——商隱之母親，年四十餘歲，生有四女三男，商隱為其長子，上有三姊，一夭折，二

商隱居右處，其母居左處，堂屋內簡單鄉間桌椅，可供坐談飲酒，長几供讀書、寫字、鼓瑟之用。

二、第二幕：長安皇宮內輕鳳寢宮，正中置門供出入，門外有走廊，台上右方有一門通臥室，屋內有桌椅、長几可供道士唸經，點香燭、燒符、放供品，另有長几，供鼓錦瑟用，另有宮殿大圓柱、布幔、宮燈等飾物，有皇宮氣氛。

三、第三幕：李商隱長安居處，台右為進出入大門，台左有門通內屋，有古色古香窗櫺，傢俱陳設較有城市氣派，太師椅、燭台，及書架，有書卷氣，牆上可掛字畫。

四、第四幕：離宮輕鳳居處，與皇宮內居處，略有不同，格子窗可看見屋外之山水景色，門外有迴廊，屋內有櫃子、抽屜櫥及梳裝台，大門外可見羽林軍站崗情景，宮殿之圓柱、布幔、香爐、宮燈、道具可與上景通用。

早嫁，李父於商隱十歲時去世，獨力照顧一家子女長大，頗為能幹，略通詩書。

李慶宇──商隱之小弟，二人相差七歲左右，出場時，約十六歲至廿歲。

令狐綯──是商隱恩公令狐楚之二公子，與商隱共遊同讀，一起長大，二人有很好的友誼，是富家子弟，服裝華麗，談吐有禮。

劉從政──是商隱在玉陽山學道時之師父，道教中人，穿道士服唸經，作法趕鬼，有模有樣，十足道教中人。

田中尉──神策軍之軍官，狐假虎畏型人物。

神策軍──兵丁多人。

家　丁──令狐綯家傭僕二人。

盧輕鳳──唐文宗之宮嬪，與商隱同年，愛好文學，天真可愛，有高貴之氣質，其處境之寂寥，令人憐愛同情。

盧飛鸞──輕鳳之親姊姊，年略長一歲，但較成熟穩重，常理智應對一切，不會過份衝動。

彩　玉──輕鳳身邊之貼身宮女，約十七八歲，機伶輕俏。

楊賢妃──唐文宗寵愛的愛妃，面善心惡，有蛇蠍美人，笑面虎之稱，年約卅歲，體弱、陰狠在骨子裡。

殷公公──楊賢妃身邊之宦官，約四十餘歲，奴才型。

來

喜——侍候鳳娘娘的小黃門，年約十五、六歲。

李執方——金吾將軍，年約四十餘歲，有鬍子，不穿盔甲上場，為人熱心，有長者風。

羽林軍——四、五人左右，穿羽林軍服裝。

序　幕

時：唐宣宗大中十二年冬。（公元八五八年）

景：李商隱家，冬天下雪，樹枝有積雪。

人：李商隱四十七歲，白髮蒼蒼，面容蒼老，韓畏之，亦四十餘歲，卻精神抖擻。

幕啓時：

二人相對坐在屋內，桌上有酒、小菜，在對酌，屋外有飄雪。

商隱放下酒杯，鼓瑟吟詩。（音樂起）

商：（吟起「錦瑟」詩來）「錦瑟無端五十弦，一絃一柱思華年，莊生曉夢迷蝴蝶，望帝春心託杜鵑。滄海月明珠有淚，藍田日暖玉生煙，此情可待成追憶，只是當時已惘然。……」（嘆息聲）唉，……已惘然……

韓：義山，你又想起了什麼難忘的往事，……在這下雪的夜晚，不妨暢開胸懷，……好好的聊一聊！

……

商：（沉緬往事）畏之，時間過得真快，一眨眼，廿多年，就這麼飛也似的過去了，還記得當年我們初相識的時候，還只是廿多歲的小伙子，如今，卻已兩鬢斑白，垂垂老矣。

韓：義山，你今年才四十七歲，怎麼可以說垂垂老了呢？

商：畏之兄，我倆是同科進士，可是，我的仕途，卻不如你的順利，我的家庭，也不如你的幸福，廿

多年的變化，……太大了，使我身心交疲，可能不久人世了。（遠處歸鴉飛過聲）

韓：義山，……你怎麼老氣橫秋，說這樣的話呢？……記得，你廿歲時，曾上玉陽山，去學過「道」，如

今，人到了中年，卻又忽然信起「佛」來？……我聽說，你經常去廟裡唸經、參禪、禮佛，是嗎？

商：是啊，我在東川的時候，專誠拜了「知玄大師」為師，聽他講解佛經，深感自己這一生，……眞

是罪孽深重。尤其是……年輕時候，那一段往事，盤踞在心裡，……隔得越久，越難以忘懷……

韓：義山，既然如此，切在知交，又是連襟的份上，何不一吐為快。

商：（考慮了一陣，舉杯向韓）畏之，……那……要怎麼說呢？……（稍頃）……先乾了這一杯！

韓：好，乾了這一杯！（二人乾杯）

商：……這些陳年往事，說出來，心裡也許會好過些，……只是（嚴肅的）務請你要代我保守秘密，

韓：好，……我絕不說出去！

商：……答應我別說出去！……

韓：好，……我絕不說出去！

（配音樂瑟聲起），燈光漸暗，幕漸下，黑暗中，商隱的述說繼續著，直至第一幕開始）

商：……記得那……一年，是太和九年，我廿四歲，已離開了玉陽山，不再學「道」，決心發憤苦讀，再

次參加進士的考試，謀取功名，……朝廷上，卻發生了血腥屠殺，駭人聽聞的「甘露之變」，…

……畏之，你不記得了嗎？

韓：好可怕的「甘露之變」，真像一場噩夢，我怎麼會不記得呢！

（配兵器打鬥搏殺聲，慘叫聲）

（急驟，慌亂的音效升起）

（幕徐徐降下）

序　幕

第一幕

時：唐文宗太和九年冬天（公元八三五年）甘露事變後不久，序幕前廿三年。

景：李商隱家。

人：李商隱、李母、韓畏之、李慶宇、令狐綯、劉從政、僕人、神策軍田中尉、神策軍兵丁多人。

幕啓時：

　是下午時分，已沒有在下雪了。

　場上已無商隱、畏之，只見李母在打掃庭院。

　掃了一陣子，再收拾桌上序幕留下的酒杯、碗筷、擦拭桌子。

　這時，小弟慶宇，氣喘吁吁的自外推開竹門進入，返身把門關好，奔向母親稟告。

母：慶宇啊，……怎麼這麼早，就收工回來啦！

宇：娘，……你……

母：不好了，……胡大爺家出事了？……

宇：出什麼事？……你快說呀！

母：胡家大少爺，……說他父親是朝中的叛逆，……和當朝的大臣賈餗（音速）有交往，……爲了斬草除根，……他兒子、孫子，也難逃一死……家財全都被充公了！……

宇：胡家大少爺，……給京城來的一批神策軍給帶走了，……說他父親已經被腰斬示衆，……他父親是朝中的叛逆，

母：胡大爺一向樂善好施，……怎麼會碰上這樣的事！……真是天下要亂了！……

宇：我聽街上的人說，皇上，自從前兩年中風以後，行動不便，早就……管不了什麼事，現在一切全由仇士良那些宦官在掌權作主！……

母：慶宇，這麼說，這幾天，外面這麼亂，你還是少出去走動。……免得惹禍上身。

宇：娘，……我還聽說，這一次京城裡發生的「甘露之變」，是禮部侍郎李訓策動的，原意是想幫助皇上，清除那些弄權的宦官，……想不到、事機不密，反讓弄權的宦官頭子仇士良抓到把柄，倒過來挾持了皇上，……關上宮門，亂殺朝中的忠貞大臣來洩憤，……連年紀已過了七十歲的宰相王涯，也因受刑不過認了罪，被他們殺了頭。……李訓雖逃到終南山，但仍被神策軍抓到正了法，那些人的親屬，不論遠近都被處死，連三歲的孩童，也不放過，有些做官的先服毒自殺死了，還被挖了墳墓，把屍骨拿出來，丟到河裡去餵魚蝦。……娘，……你說可不可怕！……

母：這樣說起來，這個弄權的宦官頭子仇士良，……比先朝的魚朝恩還可惡！……皇上也真沒用，……盡被這些小人包圍，還能做什麼呢？……

宇：是呀，娘，……

母：對了，你的三個哥哥呢？怎麼，一個也不在家？

宇：二哥，三哥都去趙大爺家幫忙打工去了，大哥，……不是去錢大人府上抄書去了嗎？

母：他呀，為了沒有能考上進士，老是喜歡發牢騷，批評朝政，……尤其

母：我擔心的，是你大哥，……

是對那位宦官仇士良，常聽他罵他弄權亂政，比先朝的高力士，魚朝恩還跋扈，⋯⋯這些話若被

人傳了開去，⋯⋯也拿他當叛逆來辦，⋯⋯那就慘了！

宇：娘，⋯⋯大哥沒做什麼官，⋯⋯我們家又沒有什麼錢，⋯⋯不用害怕！⋯⋯沒人會注意他的！

（正談說間，傳來一陣急迫的敲門聲）

（緊張的音效升起，母子張惶失措）

母：慶宇，不忙開門，⋯⋯不會是神策軍上門來抓人了吧！

宇：（膽怯的上前）請問，是誰？

韓：（門外）小弟，是我呀，⋯⋯你大哥在家嗎？

母：（鬆了一口氣）是韓公子，⋯⋯慶宇，去開門。⋯⋯

（慶宇開門，迎韓畏之入，注意韓改年輕裝扮，服裝也要換過）

韓：伯母，您好，⋯⋯義山，在家嗎？

母：韓公子，我家老大，他不在家，⋯⋯也許一會兒就回來了，⋯⋯你請坐，⋯⋯慶宇，快去錢大人

府上，把你大哥叫回來。⋯⋯

宇：是，娘，⋯⋯我這就去。⋯⋯（下場）

母：（為韓倒了杯茶送上）韓公子，⋯⋯請用茶。⋯⋯坐。

韓：伯母，不用客氣。⋯⋯今兒我來，是有個消息，⋯⋯要告訴義山。⋯⋯

母：什麼消息？……可以告訴我嗎？

韓：伯母，以義山的聰明才智，考取進士，……應該是垂手可得的，……怎麼會考了兩年，都落榜呢？……

節：要嘛，事先找人去「行卷」！

母：……伯母，你也許不清楚，當今官場有些陋習，要想考上進士，……要嘛向主考官送銀子，打通關

母：噢，……原來是這樣的！

韓：伯母，你知道去年，那個叫裴思謙的，怎麼會考上狀元的嗎？

母：我那會知道！

韓：「行卷」，就是想考進士的舉子，先把自己作的詩文，求教於當朝的王公大人，請他們看了以後，為之吹噓一番，向主考官推荐，這才有登弟的機會，否則……想都別想！……

母：「行卷」？……什麼叫「行卷」？

韓：「行卷」？什麼叫「行卷」？

韓：我最近聽人說：他是靠著宦官仇士良的關係，向主考官高鍇高大人，打了招呼，……才高中狀元的！

母：仇士良，連考狀元，他都管得着嗎？

韓：傳說仇士良，跟高鍇都講明了，不但要保證考取，而且還非中「狀元」不可，……高大人，還敢不聽從嗎！……

母：照這樣說起來，義山，……也不用再去考試了！……

韓：伯母，……你也不用洩氣。我聽說那位主考官高鍇高大人，和義山的恩師令狐楚的二公子令狐綯，很熟悉，還常有來往，而義山和令狐綯又是多年相交的好友，託他在高大人面前「行卷」、「推荐」的話，……我想明年「春試」，準可以「金榜題名」！……

母：韓公子，……眞是這樣嗎？……

韓：只要義山肯開口，……我可以保證，……他一定可以如願以償！只是，我擔心義山的個性，……

母：……他恐怕不願意這樣做！……

韓：等他回來，……我來跟他說！……這件事……對義山來說，……眞是太重要了！……

母：對了，我還忘了告訴伯母一件事，……您也該，……好好勸勸義山，……眼前，……仇士良的耳目，到處都有，外面人心惶惶，人人自危，……神策軍到處亂殺無辜，義山還是謹言慎行，明哲保身重要，千萬別再隨便亂寫些不合時宜的「詩」，……為自己找麻煩！……

韓：韓公子，……最近寫了什麼不合時宜的詩？……我一點都不知道！

母：義山，……自從朝廷發生「甘露之變」以後，……這十幾天來，朝中一些忠貞不二的大臣，都被無辜的斬殺了六、七百人之多。賈餗、王涯、李訓、刑部侍郎舒元輿都被因此腰斬送了命！……連地方上，一些有錢的富戶，和朝中官員有交往的親友，也被株連，遭了池魚之殃！……想不到義山，竟還寫了二首議論的詩，說甘露事變，人神共憤，深望天子清除奸佞，以安天下人心！……這若是讓仇士良知道了，不太「危險」了嗎？

母：（駭極）唉！……（頓足）這孩子……怎麼這樣不知輕重！……可以寫這樣的詩呢！……不知他

放在那兒，……趕快燒了才好！

韓：伯母，……他寫給我看以後，我隨手就把它撕了，……不知道，他有沒有拿給別人去看！……

母：商隱，這孩子……凡事，喜歡仗義執言，……唉，……這樣的個性，遲早會出亂子！……

（正說時，慶宇與義山自外回家，上場後慶宇到後房去，下場。義山改年輕裝扮，服裝與序幕不

同）

商：娘，……您怎麼啦？……你很少看我寫的「詩」的！

母：娘，……畏之兒，……勞你久等了！……

母：商隱，方才韓公子說，你寫了二首議論「甘露之變」的詩，……放在那裡，……快拿來，給

我看。……

商：娘，……您怎麼啦？……你很少看我寫的「詩」的！

母：快去拿來，少廢話。

商：（自書架上找出詩稿呈上）娘，……在這兒。……

母：（接過詩稿，仔細看了一遍，將之撕個粉碎）……

商：（驚訝）娘，……您……怎麼把它撕了？……

母：娘，……是為了保住你這條小命，才撕的，……你只是逞一時之快，……不怕那些神策軍，把你

抓去，砍了你的腦袋嗎？

商：娘，……孩兒是心有不平，……，有感而發！……

韓：義山，際此人心惶惶之日，……伯母，全是爲了你的安危著想！……

商：畏之兄，……就是爲我寫的這兩首詩而來的嗎？……

韓：義山，……你我兄弟，是無話不談的，……你的個性，心思，……我完全了解，……年青嘛，免不了年少氣盛，……但是，這兩首詩，一旦，落入奸人之手，……那就惹火上身，……後悔莫及了！……

商：畏之兄，……我自己寫的詩，……我願意爲之負責！……

韓：義山，……我是一片好意，……才來奉告的，……天色不早。我告辭了，……改天，……再來找你聊，……伯母，……再見。

母：韓公子，謝謝你的好意，……不送了。……

商：（目送韓離去）畏之，……改天，我去看你。……

（韓走後義山送出門外，將門栓上，母叫住義山）

母：商隱，……你先坐下，娘有話要和你說。

商：娘，……（坐下）……還有別的吩咐嗎？……

母：商隱，韓畏之，方才說，主考官高錯高大人，和令狐綯很熟悉，常有來往，你若真想考取進士的話，可以拜託令狐綯，在高大人面前「行卷」、「推荐」，……明年「春試」，就一定可以

「高」中……

商：娘，雖說，子直和我是知無不言的好友，但是，為了考取功名，要我專誠去京城，拜託他，向主考官高大人「行卷」推荐的話，……我是絕不會開這個口的！

母：商隱，你知道，去年，那個裴思謙，是怎麼會考上狀元的嗎？……他就是……派人，向高大人，……打通了關節！……

商：娘，……別人怎麼做，我沒法去管，……要我為了自己想考取功名，……去走旁門左道……我李義山，絕不去做！

母：你去試一試，也不行嗎？……子直，他不會笑你的！……

商：娘，……您別說了！……我不想去「試」，……真要這樣做，……成功了，……我也一輩子會抬不起頭來的！

母：（嘆息）唉，……商隱，你這樣不肯低頭的倔脾氣，將來吃虧的，還不是你自己。……

（此時，突門外傳來了一陣搥門聲）

田：（在門外）快開門，……聽見沒有？……

商：（上前問）誰？……

田：我姓田，……是神策軍的，……快開門呀！……

（母聞聲，急拉商隱，去後面躲一下，他不聽，非但不躲，反挺身去開門，田中尉及兩名神策軍

士進入。慶宇聞聲自內出，上場）

商：請問，軍爺，……有何公幹？……

田：奉了，右驍衛大將軍仇士良之命，前來搜捕叛逆餘黨！……（命令手下）快進屋去搜！

兵：是。……（分別推開商、母、宇等人，進入內屋）

母：（跪下哀求），民婦家孤寡渡日，……一貧如洗，……那會勾結朝中的叛逆？……

田：起來，別來這一套。（母起立）

（二兵士先後自內屋走出）

兵甲：稟告中尉，……內屋並無他人！

田：（問甲）仔細搜查過了嗎？

兵甲：仔細搜查過了。

田：（問乙）你怎麼說？……

兵乙：箱櫥，都搜遍了，……藏不住人！……

田：你們說實話，……姓什麼？……

商：姓李，十八子李。……

田：（奸笑）好極了！……我就是要找姓李的，……（手指義山）你叫什麼名字？

商：（不卑不亢）我名商隱，字叫義山。……

田：說實話，，……你跟「李訓」，……是什麼關係？

商：在下與李訓，雖爲同宗，……但素不相識。……

田：有一個名叫宗密和尚的，……是不躲在這兒？

商：是終南山的主持宗密高僧嗎？……他是個出家人！……怎麼可能躲在這兒呢？……

田：他是李訓的餘黨，……聽說已逃下終南山，躲了起來，……李訓，那個挑起「甘露事變」的叛逆，我們已經砍了他的腦袋，宗密和尚，也休想逃得出我們神策軍的手掌心！……

商：軍爺，……李訓經已伏法，……宗密和尚乃是一出家之人，……慈航普渡，……你們何不放過了他！……

田：嘿！（冷笑）你倒說得輕鬆，……要我們放過了他！……（突然發現地上撕碎的詩稿，撿拾起來，拚湊著看）

（緊張音效升起）

田：（邊看拚紙，邊唸出）……「古有清君側，……今非乏老成……」這是什麼意思？……

母：軍爺，……這是孩子們寫了丟棄不要的字紙，……你看，……都撕碎了，……還沒掃走，……您千萬別誤會！……在意啊！慶宇，……還不快拿掃帚來，把地掃一掃！……

田：（取掃帚來掃地，母欲取去田爺手上的碎紙，田不給）

宇：是，娘！（取掃帚來掃地，母欲取去田爺手上的碎紙，田不給）

田：想不到，「甘露事變」以後，朝廷上，有人不怕死，向皇上上了奏章，要「誓死清君側」，……

如今，在民間，……也有人寫出：「清君側」的詩句，來唱和！……（走至義山面前）你老實說，……

……這詩句是不「宗密和尚」所寫？他一定就在這附近窩藏著！……你若能向我供出他的藏身之處，……

……我不爲難你。

商：宗密和尚，藏身在那裡？我不知道。……方才你們不是已經仔細搜查過了嗎？……他眞的不在這

兒。軍爺，何不再逐戶查問呢？……

母：是啊，……軍爺，……我們眞的不知情！……

田：好，……我會繼續去逐戶搜查的。……不過，……這首詩，……一定也不是他寫的囉？……那

……是誰寫的？

（氣氛凝重）

宇：（代哥認罪，壯膽上前）是我隨手寫的，……寫的不好，我把它撕了！……

田：（懷疑，打量其年紀）你隨手寫的！……你是誰？你再寫一遍給我看！……

宇：（爲難地）……

商：小弟，……走開。……是我寫的，……有感而發，……可是，……這不已經……撕了嗎？……

田：你承認是你寫的詩，……很好，……大丈夫，敢做就敢當！……來人哪！……將他帶回去問話！

兵甲：是。……（二人上前欲押商走）

母：（急，上前哀求攔住）軍爺，……求你放了他，……我兒子……他年輕不懂事，……您千萬別認

眞：……

田：公事公辦，……我不能不認眞，……（推開母）老太婆，滾開，……別擋路！

宇：（上前拉住）大哥！……

（兵甲、乙仍欲押走商，正此時，忽聞敲門聲，有馬車鈴聲響起，馬蹄在竹門外停住，……）

母：慶宇，……快去看看，門外誰來了！……（宇奔去開門）

（兩個僕人抬了箱盒，禮物，還有食米麻袋自外進入）

僕人：李家公子，在家嗎？……

宇：（奔入）娘，……大哥，……令狐家的二哥來了！……

商：是令狐家的綯哥來了嗎？（高興的欲掙脫迎客，但仍被拉住。田肅目外望，僕人等將禮物送入堂屋內放下後退出，這時身穿錦衣官服的令狐綯，自外進入，看見田及兵丁，訝異地問母）

綯：伯母，……您好，……義山，……怎麼？……發生了什麼事？……

母：子直，……你來得正好，……這位軍爺，……有一點誤會，……要將商隱帶走問話呢！……

綯：啊，……什麼誤會？……

商：（摔開兵丁的手）子直兄，……我來給你介紹，……這位是神策軍的田中尉，……奉命來搜捕與叛黨李訓有交往的宗密和尚，……這位是我恩師令狐楚將軍的二少爺令狐綯公子。……令狐楚將軍，如今在朝廷官居左僕射，在中書省皇上身邊參決機務重任，軍爺，與之相識否？

田：（知來者官位不低，立即改了口吻）令狐公子，卑職久仰令尊大名，無緣相識，……真是失敬失敬。……

絢：……

田：田中尉，……不用客氣，……小弟甫自京城來，路途上風聞神策軍四出搜捕朝廷叛逆餘黨，……十分辛苦，……摯友義山，自幼與小弟一塊兒長大，……想必定是冒犯了閣下，……才有所誤會！……

田：那裡，……沒什麼！……卑職，只是奉命追捕宗密和尚，……才有所造次，……李公子，……希勿見外，……令狐公子，卑職還得去別處搜查，……恕在下失禮，告辭了。……（向兵甲、

乙）別為難他，……我們走吧！

（田放過商隱，率神策軍等出門下場）

絢：義山，……方才，究竟是怎麼回事？……

商：我只是看不慣那些宦官的作為，隨筆寫了兩首詩，……想不到會引起這些麻煩！

絢：你剛正不阿的個性，我最清楚，……可是，這年頭小人得勢，……還是慎言謹行，才好。……

母：子直，……真過意不去，每次你來，……都帶這麼多東西來，……

絢：伯母，……只是些日常用品，……也是家父我送來，……

母：令尊近來福體還康泰吧？

絢：謝伯母關心，家父，近來還粗安，他這次要我帶了封信來，……希望義山，能擺脫一切，早日去

興元府，給他幫忙，……他年歲大了，……有些文案，希望義山去代為處理。（說著身邊取出一封信交給商，商接信後閱讀。）

母：可是商隱，還一直不肯死心，希望能考取了進士，……才去興元府。……子直，……我聽別人說，您跟那位主考官高鍇高大人，情誼甚篤，便中，……不妨代商隱美言幾句……

商：娘，……這些事，……就不用你操心了！……

絢：義山，……你若果真有此意，……我……代為行卷推荐，也很方便的。

商：不，……子直，……千萬別這樣，……我希望一切順其自然。

絢：義山，……去興元府的事，你考慮得怎麼樣？……

商：謝謝令尊的美意，……我想，……還是等過了明年「春試」，……再說吧！

絢：義山，你最近可有上玉陽山去？……

商：怎麼？子直，你想去玉陽山學道？

絢：你別誤會，我只是聽你說過，玉陽山上風景悠美，道觀眾多，尤其是「聖女祠」、「華陽觀」，遠近聞名，際此天氣晴朗，想邀你作嚮導，陪我登高一遊，如何？

商：那些「道觀」，有什麼好遊覽的。

絢：義山，真人面前不說假話，難道那位宋華陽女道士，你也不想再見了嗎？

商：子直，……別再提她了，……她早已變了心，……把我忘了。……

絢：是嗎？

商：世間，「眞情」太少了，……可遇而不可求啊！（感嘆不已）

絢：這麼說，……我好不容易，抽空來邀你同遊玉陽山的事，是落空了！

商：子直，改天吧，……我眞羨慕你，……做了官，還到處遊山玩水，確是有福之人。

絢：伯母，……我得告辭了，改天，再來拜望。……

母：子直，你難得遠道而來，……吃了飯，再走。……我要商隱、陪你小飲一番，如何？

絢：伯母，今兒不打擾了，……有空，我還會再來的！……

商：子直，我送你。

（商送絢出門，向之揮手，不久，馬車啓程，馬蹄，吟噹聲漸遠去）

母：慶宇，商隱，來，……我們把這些東西，搬進屋去。

（三人一起動手，搬運那些日用禮品）

（這時，劉從政道士，在外叩門）

劉：（門外）請問，李義山，……在家嗎？

（慶宇去開門，迎劉進入，劉末着道士法衣）

（母察看禮物）

宇：大哥，……玉陽山的劉從政師父來看你了。（母上前招呼）

四四

母：劉師父，……快進屋裡坐，小弟，倒茶。

宇：是（倒茶送上）劉師父，請用茶。

商：（出迎）師父，……快大半年，沒見到您了，您還是老樣子，一點沒變。

劉：（就坐，喝茶）義山，這些日子，我一直念著你，……正巧路過，順道來看看你。

母：劉師父，現在，還在玉陽山修道嗎？

劉：我已經離開玉陽山了，到處走動走動。……義山……

母：劉師父，你們談吧，……我失陪了。……（拉慶宇走）慶宇，你也來，……別站在那兒，聽人說話。

（慶宇不想走，勉強隨之下）

劉：最近，……皇宮裡，大辦喪事，正到處找人，你知不知道？

商：甘露之變，聽說殺了六、七百人，……當然要大辦喪事啦！……師父，你說到處找人，是什麼意思？……難道那些神策軍亂抓人，殺的還不夠嗎？……

劉：宦官脅制皇上，濫殺忠良，是一回事，……皇宮找人辦喪事，是另一回事。

商：師父，……你越說我越糊塗了，……這不是同一回事嗎？

劉：我說的是另外一件事，前兩天，皇上最心愛的原配…王德妃死了。……

商：王德妃，也被仇士良派人殺死了？……

劉：不是的，……我聽說，是被另一位寵妃楊賢妃給氣死的。……

商：噢，……那眞是兩回事！

劉：這位被氣死的王德妃，還是東宮皇太子的生身之母，……皇上爲了表示哀悼，決定在皇宮裡建醮、大做法事，……可能也同時，爲那些被殺的大臣，唸經超度，……一時之間，找不到這麼多的道士進宮去，……所以才到處找人，……是找道士進宮去唸經！……

商：師父，我覺得天下最不公平的事，……就是一個皇帝，除了王后以外，身邊還要包圍一些妃嬪，婕妤，才人……好幾十個女人，做他的老婆，爲了爭風吃醋，……自然會勾心鬥角了。……

劉：聽說，皇宮中有不少怨女，十四、五歲就被選進了宮，一耽幾十年，到頭髮白了，還沒和皇上說過幾句話，一生的青春，……就葬送在皇宮裡！

商：這眞是可憐，……也是很荒唐的事。……

劉：咱們修道之士，……還是少說男女之事。……義山，……記得在山上學道的時候，有一次閒聊，你說，很想去皇宮見識見識，究竟是什麼模樣？……眼前，不就機會來了嗎？

（說話間，慶宇自內出，悄悄在旁聽著）

商：有什麼機會？

劉：皇宮大內做法事，需要道士，你……學過道，又會唸經，穿上道袍，跟我一起進宮，那些禁衛，會不讓你進去嗎？……

商：嗯，這倒眞是個好機會，……只是會不會給師父您添麻煩？

劉：義山，這你不用多慮！皇宮大內，爲了這次建醮作法之事，場面很大，道士希望能請到越多越好。……

……道門之事，你很清楚，戴上道冠，穿上道袍，和我一起進去，誰也不會認出來，……你是喬裝改扮的！……

商：師父，……聽您這麼說，我也心動了，……皇宮，此生還從未進去過，這可眞是千載難逢的好機會！……只是……會不會耽誤了我讀書的時間！……

母：（自內走出）義山，……我在擔心，……那位神策軍的軍爺，……把那張撕碎了的字紙，帶走了，會不會，過了一、二天，又來找你的麻煩！……不妨隨劉師父進宮去避一避，也好。……

商：（想了一想）娘，……你說得也對，……

宇：大哥，我也跟你一起進宮去，好不好？

商：怎麼？小弟，你也想跟去？

宇：劉師父，你看我可不可以打扮成小道士，跟我大哥一起進宮去，我幫你們做法事不會，打雜、跑腿，搬東西，都可以呀，……我會很小心，不會給你們惹麻煩的！

劉：師父，……他個子長得也不矮，可以帶他一起去嗎？……

……（打量了一下宇）……好吧，我給你去找一件小號的道袍，帶你進宮，幫忙搬運法器什麼的箱櫃，你搬得動嗎？……

宇：我力氣很大，搬得動的！

劉：好，一起去，⋯⋯不過，到了宮裡，可別隨便亂闖禁地呀！

宇：謝謝師父，⋯⋯娘，我跟大哥一起去，⋯⋯你不會不答應吧？⋯⋯

母：娘⋯⋯答應你去，⋯⋯不過，到了宮裡，什麼，都得聽劉師父的！

宇：謝謝娘！⋯⋯我去告訴二哥，三哥去！

（宇太高興了，奔出大門，去時，不小心絆倒了，跌了一大跤）

商：小心！

（劉母哈哈大笑）

（幕徐徐下。）

第二幕

時：距第一幕十天後

景：皇宮內盧輕鳳寢宮

人：盧輕鳳、盧飛鸞、彩玉、來喜、楊賢妃、殷公公、李商隱、李慶宇、劉從政

幕啟時：

盧輕鳳獨自一人在場，鼓著錦瑟、古典哀怨的曲調。香爐飄出裊裊上升的沉香，一曲將盡，彩玉自外進入，向之報告。

彩：娘娘，別鼓瑟了，……（輕鳳停止鼓瑟，起立相迎，飛鸞自外進入。）

鳳：哦，姊姊。

鸞：……我等你很久了，你怎麼現在才來。

鳳：鳳妹，……你不是說最近老是失眠，睡不著覺嗎？……我特地要御醫給你煉製了一些「安神丸」，……他說臨睡前，服用六顆，……吃完這一瓶，大概就不會再失眠了。（說著，自懷中拿出一瓶藥丸，交給輕鳳）

鸞：（接過藥瓶，看了一下，）謝謝姊姊。……（交彩玉）彩玉，……放我床邊的櫃子去。

鳳：鳳妹，……你有沒有聽到什麼傳言？……是關於王德妃突然去世的原因。（彩玉進入內屋寢室）

鳳：我聽侍女彩玉說，……王德妃娘娘，並不是自己病死的，……是有人暗中下毒手，給毒死的！……

鸞：嗯，……我也聽到這樣的傳言。……（彩玉放好藥後，自內出）彩玉，……你去門口守著，……

若是有人進來，先來通報一聲。

彩：是，鸞娘娘！（走出）

鸞：鳳妹，……你知道，……是誰下的毒手嗎？

鳳：我不知道。

鸞：我聽說是楊賢妃……身邊的殷公公，……命小黃門幹的，……真正的背後主使者，──就是楊賢

妃。……

鳳：是楊娘娘下的毒手？她為什麼要這麼做呢？

鸞：還不是想爭得皇上的寵愛，……為了拔去這根眼中釘，……她蓄意已久，……只是沒有合適的機

會吧了！……

鳳：皇上，……他知道嗎？……

鸞：皇上，……當然不能讓他知道，……這件事，……大家也只是在背後傳說，誰也找不出證據和把柄，

……這就是那位殷公公屬害的地方。……

鳳：啊，……好可怕。……

鸞：鳳妹，……我告訴你，那位楊賢妃，……是十足的「笑面虎」，……你別以為她常來找你，和你

處得很好，……實際上，不知她心裡在打什麼歪主意，……她自己沒有生育，……你和皇上，生了個皇子宗儉，……說不定，王賢妃死了以後，……她下一個目標，……就是你，……你得特別小心提防啊！……

鳳：是嗎？……姊，……（害怕）……

鸞：鳳妹，……我是你的親姊姊，……雖說，我倆同是宮嬪的身份，……但是，在皇上面前，……我是絕不會和你爭風吃醋的，……

鳳：姊，你不說，我也心裡明白！

鸞：可是，楊賢妃，她就不同了，……她是一個口蜜腹劍的蛇蠍美人，……嘴裡說得很甜，……心裡比蛇還毒！……她恨不得，皇上身邊，就只有她一個女人！……

（正說著，彩玉自外奔入）

彩：娘娘，……殷公公引着楊娘娘來了。

鸞：嘿，……說到曹操，……曹操就到了。

（殷先入，楊後上）

殷：啓稟鳳娘娘，……楊娘娘……來看你了。

（鳳、鸞，迎上）

鳳：輕鳳，恭迎楊娘娘。

鸞：飛鸞，（接著）恭迎楊娘娘。

鳳：彩玉，⋯⋯給楊娘娘奉茶。

（楊入坐，彩玉奉茶，殷公公在後站立）

楊：輕鳳，⋯⋯我是特地來⋯⋯請你去我寢宮，一起持螯賞菊，吟詩喝酒。⋯⋯飛鸞，你也來了，⋯⋯

鳳：⋯⋯就一起去吧，⋯⋯我特地準備了上好的桂花酒，⋯⋯是你們最喜歡喝的。⋯⋯

鳳：楊姐，⋯⋯您盛情邀請，⋯⋯衹是，⋯⋯一會兒，道士要來這兒唸經作法驅鬼，⋯⋯

楊：⋯⋯自當應命，⋯⋯

楊：怎麼？你請了道士，⋯⋯到你寢宮來唸經趕鬼？⋯⋯你⋯⋯遇見了鬼嗎？

鳳：我因為夜晚失眠，老是睡不著，⋯⋯自從王娘娘去世以後，⋯⋯過了三更時分，老是聽見一些窸窸窣窣的腳步聲，在屋子裡走來走去，⋯⋯昨晚還聽到一陣如泣如訴的簫聲，⋯⋯

楊：（緊張的）是嗎？⋯⋯還有簫聲？

鳳：王娘娘生前，⋯⋯最喜歡吹簫，⋯⋯我猜想一定是她陰魂不散，⋯⋯好在，這幾天，宮裡來了不少道士，在建醮做法事，⋯⋯所以，我就請了來喜，⋯⋯去醮場，請道士，⋯⋯來我這兒，唸唸經，貼幾張符咒，⋯⋯免得那些鬼魂，留連忘返，讓我寢食難安。⋯⋯

楊：輕鳳，那些道士，⋯⋯真有能力，把鬼趕走嗎？⋯⋯

鳳：這是他們的專長，⋯⋯要不然，⋯⋯皇上也用不著請他們來建醮做法事了！⋯⋯

五二

楊：嗯，……你說的也對。

（小黃門來喜率領劉道士穿法衣自外先上）

小：啟稟鳳娘娘，……作法事的劉道長已經請來了。……

鳳：有請劉道長。

劉：無量天尊，貧道劉從政叩請諸位娘娘金安。

鳳：免禮，……請坐。劉道長，我來介紹，這位是賢妃楊娘娘，這位是嬪妃鸞娘娘。

楊：劉道長，……我的寢宮，也需要你來唸經趕鬼，你有空嗎？……

（李商隱及李慶宇均穿法衣抬了一木箱進入，打開木箱，將趕鬼之香燭、香爐、桌圍、法器，一一佈置起來，並點上香燭等物，擺好瓜果供品）

劉：貧道遵命便是。

鸞：劉道長，……我也要。……

劉：貧道按序遵辦，……（問商）你……都準備就緒了嗎？……

商：都準備妥當了。

劉：那我……開始了。（打開經本，唸起經來）「蓬瀛朝爽，參禮諸天，玉清初日，鏡光圓曉，氣藹祥煙，秘典心宣，入道冀成仙。太上無極三寶大天尊。……」唸畢，搖鈴，舞劍，把符紙穿在劍上，就燭火點燃，再喝一口水，向空中噴出）

楊：輕鳳，……你忙吧，我告辭了！……飛鸞，……來，你陪我喝酒去。

鸞：鳳妹，……我走了。

（楊、鸞、殷公公先後離去）

劉：鳳娘娘，……你睡眠的臥床，……可以，容貧道進去繞床作法嗎？

鳳：是，……在這邊，……由我來帶你們進去。

（鳳引劉、商隱二人進入右邊臥房內去）

（場上僅有彩玉、及慶宇二人）

宇：姑娘，你家主子娘娘，是不是浙東人？

彩：是呀，你怎麼知道？

宇：我和我大哥，小時候，在浙東住過，……剛才我聽她的口音，……就覺得好熟悉。

彩：那個跟劉道長一起來的道長，是你的親哥哥？……你們貴姓？

宇：嗯，……他是我的大哥，姓李，木子李，……名字叫商隱，他號叫義山，我是他最小的三弟，叫慶宇。

彩：……你家主子娘娘，姓什麼？叫什麼名字？

宇：她姓盧，……是皇上的宮嬪，……我們都叫她鳳娘娘。……

彩：輕鳳，……我怎麼稱呼你呢？

宇：姑娘，……那你叫什麼名字，……

彩：她姓沈，叫彩玉，……是這兒的宮女，……你叫我彩玉就成了。……

宇：彩玉，……好好聽的名字，……（看了一下四周）啊，……這隻古琴，……是你們娘娘彈的嗎？

彩：（噗嗤笑起來）這不叫「琴」，是「錦瑟」，……鼓瑟，很好聽的唷，本來是五十根弦的，……後來，黃帝改成廿五根弦，……現在，還有十九根弦的，也有廿三根弦的！……

宇：嗄，……你懂得真不少哩！……

彩：這也是鳳娘娘告訴我的！……

（正談說間，劉道士，與商隱及輕鳳，自內臥室走出）

鳳：謝謝大法師。……

劉：義山，……等下再上香的時候，你為她唸一篇疏文、咒語，……就可以大功告成了，……好，……我先走了。……（告辭離去）

宇：是，……（為商隱點上香的……我會弄妥的。……慶宇，……上香。

商：師父好走，……我會弄妥的。……

劉：鳳娘娘，……真對不起，……前面醮場，還有不少事，等著我去處理，……我先走一步，……其餘的經文，李道長會給你唸的，……放心，……要是過了今晚，……還有什麼情況發生，……我會繼續來為你作法。……

商：（行禮後，拿劍在手，唸起疏文來）大唐文宗開成元年十月初五、浙東女弟子盧輕鳳以邇來寢宮夜半時聞怪異簫聲，特請貧道前來，上請玄天上帝、紫微帝君、二十八宿、土地使者、過往神祇，降

駕臨壇，消災降禪，……急急如律令。（唸畢、搖鈴、舞劍、噴水、）請……娘娘磕賴，上香，

「李商隱之戀」四幕舞台劇

五六

……（又忙更正）先上香，……再磕頭。……

（鳳依言上香、磕頭）

商：（收劍入鞘，收拾桌上法器等物，）啓稟娘娘，法事經已完畢，……貧道告辭了。

（慶宇繼續收拾桌上物件，一一裝入木箱中）

鳳：法師，……慢，……請等一等再收拾。

商：娘娘，還有什麼吩咐嗎？

鳳：我想請法師畫兩張趕鬼的符咒，讓我貼在房門上，這樣，到了晚間，鬼才不敢上門，……不是別的法師，都是這樣做的嗎？

商：畫趕鬼的符咒！……（輕聲地說）啊，……我別的符咒，……學過，……這趕鬼的符咒，……可把我難住了！……這怎麼辦呢？……

鳳：是否忘了筆墨，我這兒有。……彩玉，把文房四寶拿來！（彩玉入內去拿筆墨）

商：（靈機一動）啊，娘娘……我忘了帶符紙了，……慶宇，你快給我去前面醮場跑一趟，找劉師父說，娘娘，還需要兩張趕鬼的符咒，請他即刻寫一下，……好馬上拿來給我貼。

宇：是，大哥，……我這就去。（即奔下）

（彩玉自內屋取筆墨紙等文房四寶出）

鳳：道長，……從你剛才唸經做法事的種種看來，好像並非真的在道觀學道的法師，……連符紙都忘了帶來，……（正色）你……給我說實話，究竟是什麼身份，混進宮來假扮道士？……

商：我……（支吾）在玉陽山學過道，……怎麼說我是假扮的呢？……

鳳：你不說實話，……我可要叫人……把你抓起來治罪嘍！

商：娘娘既已識破，……那我也只好直說了。……在下實乃一介寒士，只是進京準備應進士試，……因過去曾在玉陽山學過一陣子道，蒙學道的劉師父帶進宮來，也只是想增長一些見識，絕無半點不良之企圖，……望請娘娘息怒，恕罪。

鳳：噢，原來是個學過道的讀書人，……，好，……既然如此，……我也不為難你，……只是，……你能把你寫的詩，……寫一首給我看看嗎？

商：娘娘，……既然有所存疑，……不才，……現在，……就寫一首，……恭請娘娘指正。

（商即就筆墨紙，當場坐下，提筆寫了一首，寫畢呈上）

鳳：（接紙，唸出所寫詩句）「嫩籜香苞初出林，於陵論價重如金，皇都陸海應無數，忍剪凌雲一片心」。……公子，這首詩的含意是否可以請你略加說明！……

商：這是我看到有人把嫩的竹筍挖出來，做菜來吃，所引起的感慨，……若是讓那些竹筍，能自然的長大成了竹林，不是更好些嗎？……

鳳：（會悟）唔，我明白了，……你是影射一些人才，……還未成長，就被人扼殺了，是嗎？……

商：娘娘，真是聰明絕頂，……一下，……就看透了我的心事！……

鳳：敢問公子，……今年貴庚？……

商：小生生於憲宗元和八年，歲在癸巳，是屬蛇的，今年虛歲是二十四歲。

鳳：（頗有興趣的追問）你是幾月出生的？

商：三月初五日。

鳳：啊，我是九月出生的，……我也屬蛇，真想不到，我們竟是同年出生。……家裡有幾個兄弟姊妹？

商：我上有三個姊姊，一個夭折，兩個俱已出嫁，下有三個弟弟一個妹妹，剛才去拿符咒的，是我的三弟，他叫慶宇，我叫義山，又名商隱。……

鳳：我沒有兄弟，只有一個姊姊，我叫輕鳳，她叫飛鸞，……比我大一歲，十年前，和我一起住在浙東，因為被官府選中，進貢送進了京城，……從此，就再也沒有走出過皇宮！……

商：娘娘在浙東長大，……難怪，你的口音，我聽起來，格外感到親切，因為，小時候，我也在浙東住過很多日子。……

鳳：是嗎？……我們，……眞有一見如故之感。……我也很喜歡寫詩，只是寫得不好！……你能寫出「忍剪凌雲一片心」的句子來，……眞使我敬佩不已。……

商：在下十六歲的時候，寫過「才論」和「聖論」的文章，當時，……曾獲得一些王公大人的讚賞，……可是如今，匆匆過了八年，……依然一無成就。……

「李商隱之戀」四幕舞台劇

五八

鳳：難怪你要拿竹箏來借題發揮了。……公子，你還年輕，……別洩氣，……我相信你是個人材，總會有出頭的一天的。

商：多謝娘娘金口。……小生若能有娘娘這樣的福氣，那就好了。……

鳳：你是不是很羨慕我在宮中的生活？……不錯，……凡是在宮外生活的人，都會這樣想。……誰又能體會到，我們終年生活在深宮中的人的苦悶和煩惱！（嘆息、哀怨）唉，……眞是不說也罷。

……

商：娘娘，怎麼這麼說呢？……民間的女子，想進皇宮裡來，比登天還難，……而娘娘在宮裡，吃的是山珍海味，穿的是綾羅綢緞，又能蒙受天子的寵愛，這還有什麼苦悶和煩惱呢？

鳳：李公子，……你是個會寫詩的讀書人，難道你沒聽說過，本朝流傳很廣「紅葉題詩」的故事。……

……一個宮女，在一片紅葉上，題下的這首詩：「一入深宮裡，年年不見春，聊題一片葉，寄與有情人」……

商：我……聽人說過這個故事，……不過，宮女，怎麼能和你娘娘來比呢？

鳳：公子，你是男人，……你不瞭解女人，……在深宮中過日子的宮女，和娘娘，其心情和痛苦，……是沒有什麼兩樣的！……

商：娘娘，……我明白你的心思，……唉，……人生本來就是苦多於樂的！

（二人心有靈犀一點通）

（慶宇拿了兩張符咒，自外進入）

宇：娘娘，……劉師父把你要的符寫好了。……他說一張貼在床架子上，一張貼在房門口，……鬼見了，就再也不會來干擾了。……

商：慶宇，……把符咒給我，……我去給娘娘貼上。……

宇：是，大哥。……（將符交給商）

（商搖著鈴，喝喝唸著經文，進入臥室，鳳，隨之入。）

（場上燈黑、暗轉）

（燈再亮時，場上木箱等已抬走，道具桌椅略有變動，顯示已過了一些時日，是夜晚，屋內已點上宮燈，輕鳳獨自在看一首詩，詩寫在一方手帕上）

鳳：（吟詩）「昨夜星辰昨夜風，畫樓西畔桂堂東，身無彩鳳雙飛翼，心有靈犀一點通」，……（放下手帕，為詩陶醉著）身無彩「鳳」（強調此字）雙飛翼，……心有「靈犀」（強調此二字）一點通……嗯，……眞寫得太好了！……

鸞：（悄悄自外進入）鳳妹，……你在房裡幹什麼？……

鳳：（急把手帕藏起來）姊，……沒什麼！

鸞：你手裡藏的是什麼？……拿來，給我看。（將手帕搶去）

鳳：是一塊手帕嗎，有什麼好看的。

六〇

鸞：（展開手帕，看見上面有題詩，順口唸了起來）「昨夜星辰昨夜風，畫樓西畔桂堂東，身無彩鳳雙飛翼，心有靈犀一點通」……嗯真是一首好詩，這字也寫得秀氣飄逸，……鳳妹，……這分明是一首情詩，……是誰寫給你的？……鳳妹！

鳳：（欲語還休）……你讓我怎麼說呢？……

鸞：鳳妹，……是不是你動了凡心？……找到了意中人？……

鳳：我也說不上來，……事情發生得太突然了，……是我做夢也想不到的事！……

鸞：鳳妹，別吞吞吐吐了，……在姊姊面前，你還有什麼需要隱瞞，不能說出來的呢？……我不會隨便……去說給別人聽的！……

鳳：姊，……我給你再看一首他寫的詩。（說著，去抽屜，取出一張紙，上寫有一首詩，交給姊看。

鸞：（唸詩）：「八歲偷照鏡、長眉已能畫，十歲去踏青，芙蓉作裙衩。十二學彈箏，銀甲不曾卸，十四藏六親，懸知猶未嫁，十五泣春風，背面鞦韆下。」……這不是說我倆小時候的故事，……十四歲離開家鄉，進入宮中以來，……就再也沒有痛快的歡笑過！……鳳妹，他究竟是誰？……你們相識多久了？

鳳：（坦述心事）自從那一天，他來我這兒，趕鬼走了以後，他的影子，就留在我心裡，怎麼趕也趕不走了！……

鸞：噢，……我知道了，……就是那個年紀輕輕，像個書生一樣的道士，對不對？……難怪你說，他

趕的鬼，……沒趕走，……三天兩頭的……要他再來給你唸經作法。……這兩首詩，……都是他

寫的？……

鳳：嗯！……姊，……再過幾天，七七四十九天的建醮法事一結束，……他就再也不可能到宮裡來了，……

鸞：鳳妹，……你要明白你自己的身份，……你是一個宮嬪，和一般的民間女子不一樣，除了皇上，……

……你心裡是不容許，有第二個男人存在的，……你知道嗎？……

……也許，……我和他，再也無法見面了。……

鳳：我知道自己的地位和處境，不允許，……我和他在一起，……可是，……我明明心裡知道，……

不能和他在一起，……但是，……我做不到，……我好苦啊！……

鸞：你知道就好，……做完了法事，……你就把他忘了吧！……不要跟自己過不去，自尋

煩惱了。……一個道士，犯不著你這樣為他六神無主的，……

鳳：姊，……他並不是真的道士，……他是個未考上進士的讀書人，……憑他的才學，智慧，假以

時日，我相信他會考上進士，……出人頭地的！

鸞：（苦苦相勸）鳳妹，別胡思亂想了，……忘了他吧！

鳳：我……是想忘了，……可是，忘不了……真的，忘不了。……

鸞：……就算他考取了，做了進士，……又能怎樣呢？……他出人頭地，難道他會做「皇上」嗎？……

……唉！……宮裡面，嬪妃不只有你一個，……大家都互相在監視著，……稍有不慎，……

……那是不可能的事！……

……就會有一些風言風語，流傳出去，……若是傳到了皇上的耳朵裡去，……他一發起火來，……那就麻煩大了，……到那時候，……姊姊縱想護著你，怕也救不了你，……你明白嗎？

鳳：姊，……你說的這些，我都懂，……可是，……我心裡就是放不下，老是在唸叨著他……爲了他，我飯也吃不下，覺也睡不好。

鸞：鳳妹，你年紀也不算小了，……聽姊姊的勸，沒錯，……千萬別糊塗的走錯了一步，……俗話說：「一失足成千古恨」，……到時候，再後悔也沒用了。……啊，時間也不早了，……我去睡了，……你也早點睡吧！……明兒見。……

鳳：明兒見。

（鸞走了，鳳看著手帕，想思重重，獨自拿起錦瑟來鼓奏著）

（稍頃，彩玉自外進入，悄悄走向鳳）

彩：啓稟娘娘，……（神秘地）李公子，……他來了。

鳳：（停止鼓瑟）彩玉，……他真的來了？

彩：嗯。……（引李商隱進入，李改穿內侍服裝）

鳳：你在外面守著，若有人經過，……就給我咳嗽一聲。……

彩：是，娘娘，（退下）

商：沒有想到，……你的瑟，還鼓得這麼好。……

鳳：沒有你的詩寫得好，……早知道，我該改叫「彩鳳」，……才對。……

彩：娘娘，……彩鳳，……就是我心目中的「輕鳳」，……娘娘，……從今晚起，我能叫你的芳名，「輕鳳」嗎？……

鳳：好呀，……我也不再叫你義山，……我叫你商隱，……希望你真是一個隱士，在宮裡……誰也看不見你，……除了我。……

商：輕鳳，……建醮的法事，馬上就快結束，……今晚也許是我最後一次來見你，……以後，我這一生，恐怕，再也不能和你見面了！

鳳：商隱，別說這樣感傷的話，……只要你願意，我想，……我們還是可以想法子暗中聯絡，時常見面的！

商：是嗎？……皇宮禁衛森嚴，我插翅也難飛入禁地啊！

鳳：對了，……剛才，小黃門來喜領你來的時候，有沒有被人發現？

商：我是從小閣、斜門，穿過迴廊走來的，……加上穿了內侍的衣服，……怎麼會被人發現，……我記得，你的寢宮前，有幾棵桂花樹，只要聞著桂花的香味走，……大概就不會走錯。

鳳：你呀，……真聰明。

商：不，你比我更聰明。……在我這一生，還沒遇見過，比你更聰明的女子，你看，你不但會養蠶、織絹、裁衣，還會焙藥、搗藥、擦玉、磨犀……更難得的，是會作詩、唱曲、鼓瑟、舞蹈，……

天下，能會這麼多才藝的女子，……也沒幾個吧？

鳳：（樂不可支）你眞會說話……這些本事，是我十三、四歲進宮以後，近十年的磨練，慢慢一樣一樣學會的，也沒什麼稀奇。

商：你這樣說，我可不這樣想，……若是十個才女加起來，也抵不上你一個。

鳳：你呀，……把我說得「太」好了。……

商：輕鳳，我……說的全是出自肺腑的眞「心」話！……

　　（二人相依偎在一起）

鳳：對了，……商隱，在曲江，皇上有個「離宮」，你有沒有聽說過？

商：皇上有個「離宮」，在曲江那兒？我不清楚吔！

鳳：距離長安東南十里遠，皇上的「離宮」，也就是皇上的「別館」，每當春天來的時候，……皇上，會帶我們這些妃嬪，去那兒小住，……那兒最近經過了一番整修，風景眞是美極了，煙水明媚，南有「芙蓉園」，西臨「慈恩寺」、「杏園」，一到春天，百花齊放，萬紫千紅，人在那裡，就像進了圖畫一樣。

商：你這一說，我想起來了，每年皇上擺筵席，宴請那些新科狀元，和新貴人的地方，就在那兒，對不對？

鳳：對，……「離宮」那邊的門禁，不像皇宮這樣森嚴周密，負責巡查的羽林禁衛，人數也有限，……

商：到了「離宮」，……我們就可以經常會面，不會有人知道的！

鳳：輕鳳，……真太好了，……什麼時候，你們才搬到「離宮」去住呢？

商：……我方才不是說了嗎，……要到春天，……現在是暮秋，……至少還要過三個月。

鳳：三個月，……（用手指來計算）一個月卅天，三個月要九十天，啊，……好漫長的日子，……我真恨不得，明後天，你們就搬到「離宮」去住。

商：瞧你，……急成這個樣子！

商：輕鳳，……有人說：「一日不見，如隔三秋」，如今，我們要分開九十天，……那要隔多少個秋？……過去，在我的生活中，除了讀書，抄書，……日子過的好慢，……也無絲毫的樂趣可言，……如今，……認識你以後，……心靈上有了寄託，……覺得活得好愉快，……但是，……偏偏就不能常在一起。……

鳳：商隱，……過去，我在養蠶的時候，時常在想，我跟那養的蠶一樣，生下來，就是被人用桑葉飼養長大，……到了有一天，吐絲結成了繭，把自己困在裡面，……這樣活著，究竟有什麼意思呢？

商：輕鳳，……別太感懷身世了，蠶也會有破繭而出的一天，蠶後代的生命，還等待靠她去延續完成呢！

鳳：商隱，我們的交往，也會有這樣的一天嗎？

商：會有這麼一天的！輕鳳，……你看，今夜的月色多美，……月宮裡的嫦娥，也在羨慕我們呢！

（二人正陶醉依偎著，忽聞外面彩玉的咳嗽聲）

鳳：（驚覺）啊，不好了，……有人來了，……

商：有人來了，……那怎麼辦？……

鳳：你……快進我臥室去躲一躲，……千萬別出來。……

（商匆匆入內）

彩：（自外進入）娘娘，……殷公公陪著楊娘娘來看你了。……

殷：（先入，向鳳行禮）鳳娘娘，……楊娘娘，……來看你了。……

（楊在後入）

鳳：輕鳳，恭迎楊娘娘，……

楊：免禮。

鳳：彩玉，……給楊娘娘奉茶。……

彩：是。（去倒茶，楊已入坐）

鳳：楊娘娘，……深夜駕臨，……有什麼重要的吩咐嗎？……

楊：（若無其事，但遊目四顧）輕鳳，……也沒什麼事，……我啊，……是皇上不在身邊，……深夜輾轉不能成眠，……是來找你聊天，解悶的。

鳳：噢！⋯⋯（鬆了一口氣）⋯⋯

楊：輕鳳，⋯⋯我有不少的心事，⋯⋯想和你談，⋯⋯今晚，我就睡在你這兒，抵足而眠，談個痛快，可以嗎？

鳳：（緊張）娘娘，⋯⋯我，⋯⋯睡覺會打鼾，⋯⋯恐怕，⋯⋯不太好吧？⋯⋯

楊：沒有關係，⋯⋯我，⋯⋯也會打鼾！⋯⋯殷公公，⋯⋯你進去看看，⋯⋯先把枕頭被褥，給我舖好。⋯⋯

鳳：娘娘，⋯⋯由我去舖好了，⋯⋯不用麻煩殷公公了。⋯⋯（阻殷入內）

殷：不，⋯⋯這是奴才份內的事。⋯⋯（仍欲入內）

楊：（向殷使以眼色，目的在搜查）讓殷公公去做吧，⋯⋯這是他該做的！

（殷進入臥室，鳳緊張萬分，情急智生）

鳳：啓稟娘娘，⋯⋯

楊：輕鳳，⋯⋯你想說什麼？

鳳：我這臥室，雖說已經道士作法唸經，可是，⋯⋯半夜裡，依然陰風陣陣，有時候，還可聽到女鬼的嚶泣聲，⋯⋯我怕嚇著娘娘，⋯⋯還是請娘娘回自己寢宮去安息，比較放心。⋯⋯

楊：（拖延）哦！⋯⋯是女鬼呢？還是男鬼啊？⋯⋯

鳳：娘娘，⋯⋯你不怕鬼？⋯⋯

殷：（自內室出）娘娘，被褥舖好了，……可以進去安息了。……

楊：（言外有意）你……你……沒有發現……什麼「不乾淨」的……東西吧？……

殷：被褥、枕頭、床單、蚊帳……都……很乾淨啊！……

楊：（考慮有頃）……你說得也對，……我還是回自己寢宮去睡，比較好，……你安息吧，……我回去了！……殷公公，……帶路。

殷：是，……娘娘。

（殷先出，楊隨後出）

鳳：啊，……好險！

（鳳抹去額頭上的冷汗）

商：幸好，……我躲在衣櫃裡，……差一點，……

（商隱衣冠不整，自內屋出走）

彩：李公子，……若被發現，就沒命了。

（二人驚嚇中，幕急落下）

第三幕

時：開成二年春至夏

景：李商隱長安居處

人：李商隱、李母、李慶宇、韓畏之、令狐綯、李執方、來喜

幕啓時：

京城附近的民房，大門通外面在左上方，右方有門通內室，室內佈置有書卷氣。古色古香的窗欞，窗外有樹木花香。屋內傢俱陳設，較第一幕有氣派，太師椅、茶几，有書桌、燭台，及放線裝書的書架。李母一人在場上抹拭書架。慶宇穿著整潔的，自外進來。

母：慶宇……

宇：娘。

母：慶宇，自從你大哥，今年春天，考取了進士，我們家搬到京城來以後，你和你大哥，經常一起進城去玩，……究竟城裡，有那些好玩的地方，讓你們哥兒倆，留連忘返，……玩到很晚，才想到回家。

宇：娘，……城裡有一條曲江，風景好，可以划船、賞花，……還有不少的亭台樓閣，比起我們鄉下，……真是好玩多了，……再說，大哥最近又認識了不少新的朋友，……在一起彈琴，……鼓瑟，吟

詩，飲酒，……猜謎，藏鉤，可有趣哪！

母：慶宇，……自從咱們搬來長安以來，一些過去很少來往，住在京城的親戚，都因你大哥，考取了進士，紛紛找媒婆上門來，給你大哥提親。……

宇：嘿，……大哥沒考上的時候，……理也不理我們，……這些人，……真勢利。

母：我想你大哥已經廿五歲，該娶親了，可是，我每一次正經地和他提起這件事的時候，……他忙推

說：「不急不急，……等我考取了『博學鴻詞科』再說，」……為什麼還要等呢？……該不會是他在京城裡，已經有了中意的女人啦？……

宇：娘，你不知道，……朝廷上吏部的規定，考取了進士，……不能作數，一定還得通過「博學鴻詞科」的考試，才能派出去擔任官職，……若是通不過這一關，……還是沒法派任官職的！

母：啊，……原來是這樣！……

（這時，李商隱，換了一件亮麗的衣服，春風滿面的自外進入。……）

商：娘！（請安）

母：商隱，……你到那兒去了？……這時候，才回來。……

商：娘，……我是去李執方將軍府上，……和他下了一盤棋，所以，回來晚了。……（這時商與宇低

語一番，慶宇悄悄外出下）

母：是你……新認識的金吾將軍？曾到我們家來過的那一位？

商：是啊！……娘，……他是涇原節度使王茂元家的親戚，……就住在城裡招國坊，朱雀街東的第三

街，……房子好大，……大廳、書房、迴廊、廂房，陌生人走進去，……不小心，真會迷路呢！

母：……

商：他雖是一個將軍，……但是一點官架子都沒有，平易近人，……和我雖是初交，……但我們談得

很投機，……他還說，改天，……他要介紹王茂元節度使，……和我見面認識呢？……

母：喔！……那個有錢又有勢的王節度使，……如今可是朝廷上的大紅人呀！

母：嗄！……你和李將軍……很談得來嗎？……

商：畏之兄，……瞧你喜氣洋洋的，……今兒，……來找我有什麼事嗎？

韓：義山，……我今兒是專誠來給你送喜帖的，……下個月初十，……是我的大喜之日，（說着自懷

中掏出一張紅帖送上）……你我是同科進士，……一定要大駕光臨，喝我這杯喜酒呵！

（正談說間，韓畏之自外進入）

韓：伯母，……您好。義山，……你正巧在家，……沒出去啊？……

母：韓公子，……你們聊，……我有事，失陪了，……（入內下）

商：（又驚又喜）什麼？……你怎麼不吭不響的，……說娶親就娶親，可真把我嚇了一大跳！……新

韓：娘子是誰家的千金啊！……能和你匹配良緣，可真是好福氣啊！

韓：是涇原節度使王茂元家的大千金，……

商：是王茂元節度使的大千金，名門閨秀，……畏之兄，王公是當今掌兵權的豪門，家財萬貫，他願把他的大千金終身，託付於你，你可真艷福不淺啊！

韓：義山，……說正經的，……你我是好兄弟，情同手足一般，我這位岳丈共生有七位千金，除了老大，還有六位待字閨中，喜宴之日，我可以為你一一介紹相識，若有你中意的，……我來為你撮合，……若是成功了，將來，我們，不就成了連襟了嗎？

商：畏之兄，你別說笑了，王公有財有勢，如今更是朝廷上李黨中的紅人，我只是一個寒士，那有資格去高攀，……你的好意，我心領了。……

韓：對了，……義山，……我好幾次來找你，你都出去了，……那一天，我聽李執方將軍說，……你和他家人，曾同遊了一次曲江，……你知道李執方將軍和王茂元是什麼關係嗎？

商：我只聽他提起，說是親戚。什麼關係，我就不清楚了。

韓：讓我來告訴你吧，……王茂元的夫人，……是李將軍的姊姊，……也是我未來夫人的舅舅！……

商：嗄，這麼說，……你成婚之後，和李將軍也有密切的親戚關係囉！……

韓：是呀，義山，……你的恩師令狐楚，現在興元府，任山南西道的節度使，他是牛黨中的台柱，你遲早要到興元幕府去當差，而我當了王茂元的女婿，卻變成了李黨中人，……今後，咱們要像過去一樣的歡聚在一起，……可就不太容易了。……

商：（感喟的說）……唉，一個朝廷好好的，何必分成兩派，互相勾心鬥角，這樣終非國家之福，若

是大家能一條心，……不分牛黨、李黨，團結一致，共同為天下蒼生著想，那該要有多好呢？

韓：義山，……你的想法，……我完全同意，……怎奈，如今一般追逐名利之士，……卻不是這樣的想法！……

商：朋黨之爭，……這樣發展下去，……大唐天下，唉，……真是不敢想像！……

韓：不說了，義山，我還有不少別的地方要去送帖子，……我告辭了。……

商：恕我不遠送，……喜宴之日，……我一定到。……

（商送韓至門口，韓離去）

商：（自門口折回，看著喜帖，不勝羨慕之情）畏之真好福氣，……竟然，……這麼快，……就請我喝喜酒了，……而我，……什麼時候，……才可以請他喝喜酒呢！

（此時，……慶宇自外進入，手裡拿著一封信。）

宇：大哥，……這是（輕聲）「離宮」裡鳳娘娘，請小黃門來喜給你帶來的書信，說，要你看後，馬上就把它撕了。

商：（緊張的撕信來看，由輕鳳O、S幕後唸出）商隱，……原定明晚相約會晤之事，茲因皇上在「離宮」宴請群臣，所有的妃嬪，均需陪皇上去飲酒、觀舞、猜拳、作樂，故原訂之約會，只能取消，……希望鑒諒，輕鳳手啟。……

宇：大哥，……明天，……你不能去了？……

商：（失望，難過）……唉！……相見時難……別亦難！……

宇：送信來的來喜，……還特別關照說，……要大哥千萬別去冒險，……說是已經有人向上面告發，……楊賢妃，今兒白天，還特地把鳳娘娘找了去，……說要她注意自我檢點言行，……萬一出了亂子，……

……宮裡的規矩，是男的「斬首」，女的「絞死」，休想還能活命！……

商：可是，過了明晚，……鳳娘娘，……他們又要離開曲江「離宮」，回到京城宮裡去了，……也許，從此，和她再也見不到面了。……（把信片片撕碎）

宇：大哥，……見一面都這麼危險，……你還是把鳳娘娘給忘了吧！……

（這時，母自內出，悄悄躲在一邊，偷聽兄弟二人的談話。）

商：我……日夜……都在思念著她！……怎麼能說忘就忘呢？……

宇：大哥……那……你究竟有什麼打算？……

商：小弟，……你不知道，……鳳娘娘，……她……

宇：她……怎麼樣？……是真的……喜歡你嗎？……

商：她……已經把什麼都給了我了，……難道對我還不算是真心的嗎？……她願意拋棄所有的榮華富貴，和我廝守在一起，過一輩子粗茶淡飯的苦日子！……

宇：大哥，……你要明白，……她不是一個普通的女人，……她是宮中的嬪妃，……是皇上的女人，……你搶了皇上的女人，……你還要不要活命？……

商：小弟，……我們來想法子，……要綵玉、來喜他們幫忙，……幫鳳娘娘逃出宮來，……不讓皇上

給抓到，……不就成了嗎？……

宇：大哥，……別打這樣的如意算盤了，……深宮內院，你去一趟，都不容易，讓鳳娘娘逃出宮來，

……那……比海底撈針，還要難！……你真是吃了熊心豹子膽！……

商：小弟，……你別洩我的氣！……今晚，……我就冒險去闖一闖！……（欲走

宇：（急將之拉住）大哥，……你瘋了？……你絕不能拿性命去開玩笑。……

商：小弟，……放手，……別拉著我，……你讓我去！……

母：（衝出，擋住商隱去路）商隱，……你不怕死，……連你「娘」，也不顧啦？

商：娘！（怔住）我和小弟說的話。……您……都聽見了？

母：娘做夢也沒有想到，……你……竟然會愛上了一個宮裡的嬪妃，……你還想幫她逃出宮去，……

你讀了這些年的書，……連個前程安危，都不顧了嗎？

商：娘，……這不是三言兩語能說得清的，……不錯，……她是一個皇宮裡的嬪妃，……可是，她進

宮十年，芳華虛度，……毫無生活的幸福可言，……為什麼我不能搭救她飛出樊籠，……過自由

自在的新生活呢？……

母：你還敢振振有詞，……和娘來「頂嘴」？……（怒極摑其一耳光）你是昏了頭，在做白日夢！……

……你和皇上的女人，糾纏在一起，……不但你會惹上殺身之禍的，還連累全家問罪……你知不知

商：……虧你還自認是個「孝子」，……你要是為了個絕對高攀不上的女人，殺了頭，又連累一家人，……你對得起死去的爹嗎？……

（內心痛苦、愧疚、撫面頰，雙膝跪下）……娘，……我錯了！……

（舞台燈黑，暗轉）

（燈再亮時，娘已換了夏天的服裝，坐在堂屋裡憩息，手握芭蕉扇在搧著，顯示春天已過，如今是夏末秋天了）

母：慶宇，……去門口看看，是什麼貴客來了。

（慶宇點著燈在埋首讀書，也用扇子，在趕蚊子）

（稍頃，屋外有馬蹄聲傳來，在門口停下馬聲）

宇：慶宇，……開門，迎李將軍入，李穿緊身武官服裝）

（慶宇走出，開門，迎李將軍入，李穿緊身武官服裝）

宇：娘，……李將軍來了。……

（母忙出迎）

母：李執方將軍，今兒難得貴客臨門，……請進。

李：伯母，……您好。……令郎義山，……他在家嗎？

母：李將軍，真不巧，商隱他，和朋友喝酒去了，……不過，……也許過一會兒也快回來了，……慶

宇，快給李將軍倒茶。……

宇：是，娘。（忙去倒茶送上）

李：伯母，……令郎不在，也好，……我今天來，……是專程來爲令郎說媒提親的，……這件事，……

母：我想伯母，是有權可以作主的。……

李：李將軍，……但不知，……是那家的千金閨秀？

母：伯母，……在下提的是涇原節度使王茂元家的二千金，今年春天，我和令郎同遊曲江的時候，正巧與王茂元他們全家在橋上相遇，事後，……令郎和王二小姐，也曾交談過，彼此，……好像都有很好的印象。

李：呀，……對了，……商隱，好像也曾和我提起過，……不過，……王家有財有勢，……我家平民身份，……那敢高攀呀！

母：伯母，……男女婚姻，講究的是緣份，……王公雖貴爲節度使，……他有七個千金，五個少爺，……若個個都要門當戶對，才能締結成姻親，……這不大難找了嗎？……說實在的，王公是我的姊夫，……他曾坦誠的對我說，……選女婿，不在乎對方有無錢財，主要是著重在是否是個人材！……

母：李將軍，……商隱，雖說已考取了進士，……可是這一次參加「博學鴻詞科」的考試，……初試是錄取了，誰知道複試時，卻又遭無辜的被抹去了名字，……唉，他……在王公眼裡，還能算得上，是個「人材」嗎？

李：伯母，……如今的考試，……都受了一些人事上的關說，實在算不上「公正」。令郎的才氣和詩

文，……王公和在下，都是衷心讚賞，……來日必然為「棟樑」之材，……是可斷言的。……要

不，……我也不會冒昧的，來親自向你提這門親事。

母：李將軍既然這麼看重商隱，……我也就不再多說，……等他回來，我會要他考慮後，親自給你答

覆，……就這麼說定了，……可以嗎？……

李：只要伯母同意，……我想義山，……應該也會同意的，……那……我告辭了，對了，王茂公的長

女婿韓公子，……不僅是和義山同科進士，同時也是相交多年的好友，……若是這門親事結成了，他

們就成了「連襟」，……今後就更可以常在一起飲酒吟詩了！……

母：啊，……還有韓公子這層關係，……看來，……商隱，一定會同意這門親事的！……

李：伯母，……我留步，……我盼望，……這件好事，……能早一點聽到佳音。……

母：李將軍，……好走。（送李出門，不久，門外響起一陣馬蹄聲，疾馳而去）

宇：娘，……你是該給大哥定親了！……大哥若真做了王茂元家的乘龍快婿，……你還愁他，……不

能做官嗎？

母：嗯，……你說得不錯，……真成了家，……你大哥，……也才會對那位宮裡的鳳娘娘，死了這條

心。……最近這一年來，……他有沒有再偷偷去曲江，和那位鳳娘娘會面了呢？……

宇：我不知道，……

母：真不知道嗎？

宇：他現在，……去那兒，都不和我說，……就怕我，不小心，會洩漏了他的秘密。

母：……嗯，……看樣子，……他和那鳳娘娘，……還是藕斷絲連！……唉，……他怎麼會痴迷成這個樣子，……怎麼勸，都勸不醒他！……嗯，……看來，……這件婚事，我非促成他不可，……而且，……越快辦妥，越好讓我安心！……

宇：……娘，……大哥，若是娶了媳婦，……那我跟誰去睡！……我們家又這麼小，你總不會讓我去睡柴房吧！……

母：慶宇，……對了，……你二哥、三哥，還有四妹他們人呢？……怎麼，一個也不在家！……都到那兒去了？

宇：……娘，……您忘了，今兒上午，前莊周大爺家莊管家，請他們去周家莊幫忙舂米去了……恐怕，……要很晚才能回來喔！

母：……噢，……方才……，我一高興，把什麼都忘了。（茫然）

宇：娘，我想還是等大哥做了官以後……再為他成親吧！……眼前，咱們家這麼破舊，……人家是有錢人家的千金小姐，……她會樂意的來住這破房子嗎？……也許，住不了一天，……她就哭著逃回娘家去了！……

母：（考慮有頃）嗯，……你說得也對，……她是富貴人家大小姐，……怎麼會願意做咱們窮人家的

媳婦，來吃苦受罪呢？唉，這門親事……我真拿不定主意了，……（左右爲難地）究竟該同意呢？……

……還是不同意呢？……

（此時，馬車叮噹聲在門外響起停在門口）

母：慶宇，快去門口看看，……也許是令狐家的二公子來了。

（慶宇至門口，商隱面孔通紅，步履蹣跚、醉熏熏的走入，令狐絢隨後上場）

絢：小弟，……你大哥，今天酒喝多了，醉了，你扶他進房休息去吧！

商：誰說我醉了！……（打酒嗝）我心裡清醒得很！……（走路跌跌撞撞）

母：（迎上前去）子直，……怎麼，商隱，你真喝醉了！……

商：娘，……我沒醉，……只是今兒心情不太好。……稍爲多喝了幾杯？……

母：子直，……我不陪你了……你們聊吧！……（退下）

絢：小弟，……時間也不早了，……你還是扶你大哥進屋去，……早點休息，……我也得回去了。

……（欲走，但被商隱拉住）

商：子直，……你不能走，……今天，……我是喝了不少酒，……我心裡有不少的話，要和你說，……

絢：好……我不走！……義山，……你要和我……說的是什麼呢？……（坐下）

○

……（俗話說：「酒後吐真言」，……難道，你不想聽我說幾句真心話！

商：子直，……打從我十六歲寫文章，被令尊賞識任用，我倆一直玩在一起，讀書寫字也在一起，……

絢：義山，你怎麼說這些，……誰也沒說，……你是這樣的人啊！

商：我平生並不想做官，……更不想做什麼大官，……我討厭官場上的黨派之分，……為什麼要把一個好好的朝廷硬分成兩派，……不是牛黨，就是李黨，難道，……像我這樣不想捲入黨派漩渦的人，……就沒有第三條路可走嗎？……

絢：義山，……眼前的風氣如此，……不是我們個人的力量，……所能扭轉挽回的！

商：（嘆氣）嗨，……我真是「生不逢辰」，……生在這個不幸的朝代。

絢：義山，……我知道，……為了進士考試，博學鴻詞的科試，……你受了不少的委屈，……不過，……家父始終非常讚賞你的才能，……所以，一再寫信來要你去興元幕府任職！……這總不是假的吧！……

商：子直，令尊的恩情，……我終生不會忘，……你看我是個會忘恩負義的無恥之徒嗎？……別人，不瞭解我，總不成，你也對我，一點信心也沒有？……（宇自內屋出）

絢：義山，……我始終對你，有信心。……也對你的才學，……表示欽佩，……時間真的不早了，……我得回去了，……改天，……我們再聊！……（向宇）小弟，我走了，……再見。（出門而去，宇送之下）

（馬車鈴鐺聲響遠去）

（李母自內走出，宇關好大門返回）

母：商隱，……子直，他走啦？……

商：嗯。……

母：慶宇……你去睡吧！……

宇：是。（入內屋下）

母：商隱，……你……酒醒了沒有？

商：娘，……我根本沒有醉呀！……

母：那好，……娘要告訴你一件事。……剛才，你還沒回來的時候，……你認識的那位李執方將軍來

過了，……他是專誠來……為你做媒提親來的！

商：娘，……我心裡，……早有了人，……用不著……他來做媒。

母：他是一片好意，商隱，……你知道他為你做媒的對象是誰嗎？……他說你也曾見過的！

商：是誰？……（略顯緊張）

母：是逕原節度使王茂元家的二小姐，……大小姐嫁給了韓畏之，……不是你還去吃過喜酒了嗎？……

……這件婚事，若是成了，……你和畏之就成了連襟啦！

商：娘，……人家是權貴富豪之家，……而我們家這樣寒酸，……這怎麼能相配呢？……

母：我也這樣說了，……可是李將軍說了，……王茂元是他的姊夫，……他不計較，男方有沒有錢財，……
　　只要他……是個人才，……尤其是你……他對你的才學，……十分的讚賞，……看準你……將
　　來會是個棟樑之材。……

商：娘，……這門親事，……我不會同意的……你……還是回絕了吧！……謝謝他們的美意，……我
　　實在不想接受。……

母：商隱，……你考慮……也不考慮了嗎？……

商：娘，……孩兒心中，……早已有所屬，……再也容不下別的女人了！……

母：商隱，……你……還是忘不了……那個鳳娘娘？……

商：（酒意又起）娘，……孩兒不孝，……沒聽你的忠言，……希望妳能原諒。輕鳳，獻身給我的時
　　候，我曾發下重誓，此生非她莫娶，……就是為她丟了性命，……也在所不惜！……娘，……（
　　向母跪下，哭著）你就可憐孩兒，……成全孩兒這份真情！……別讓孩兒成了負心的人！……

母：（深受感動……半響）商隱……你先起來！……

商：（仍跪著）娘，……你答應了，……孩兒才起來。……

母：（嘆息）唉！……商隱，……這麼好的一門親事，別人求之不得……你卻不肯答應，一心一意，
　　要往走不通的死胡同去鑽，……娘，……怎麼忍心，……看你這樣做呢？……你這樣跪著，……
　　不肯起來，……娘的心裡……像比用刀子在割著還疼，你知道嗎？……

商：娘……

母：商隱，……你今年廿六歲了，……已經考取了進士……怎麼會為了一個女人，連性命都不顧了，……你……要為娘的，怎麼說你才好呢！……

商：（起立）好，……娘……我不勉強娘，……一定要答應我的請求，……但是，……我也求娘，別勉強我，……答應這門親事。……輕鳳給了我一片真情，我……絕不能辜負了她，……做一個沒心肝的人啊！……

母：商隱，……李將軍是你的好友，……他也完全是看重你，……才熱心好意來上門提親，……你這樣拒人於千里之外，……怎麼說得過去呢？……

商：娘，……我這些天，心理已經夠煩夠苦的了，……求娘……別再逼我了，……

母：（無奈）好，……娘不逼你，……你自己一個人，靜靜的想一想吧！……娘去睡了！……（嘆息）唉，……你心煩，……心苦……娘的心，……比你更煩……更苦呀！……（向自己房內下）

（商獨自在場上沈思著）

商：（接近桌子，看亮著的蠟燭，不免感觸萬千）唉，……可憐的蠟燭，……你比我更可憐，……你的眼淚，……什麼時候，才能流乾呢！……（吟詩句）……春蠶到死絲方盡，臘炬成灰淚始乾。

（門外傳來敲門聲）

商：好像有人在敲門？……（走向大門去，問門外的人）門外是誰？……（門外，敲門聲繼續）

喜：（門外）李公子在家嗎？……

商：（未開門）你是誰？……

喜：（門外）李公子，……我是來喜啊！……

商：（開門，見來喜著平民裝，大喜）來喜，……是鳳娘娘……要你來的？……

喜：（進入屋內自懷中取出一封信交商）公子，……是鳳娘娘，……要我交給你的……娘娘，……希
望你有空，……去看她，……她又回「離宮」來了……

商：（急忙看信）好，……我……會去的，來喜，……謝謝你。

喜：我走了，……公子，……再見。（下）

（商去關門，……母披睡袍自內出）

母：商隱，……剛才，……是誰來了？……

商：（掩飾）沒有人來呀……。

母：我好像聽見有人在和你說話？

商：啊，……是個過路的，……他迷了路，……向我問路的！

母：噢！……

（燈黑）

（幕徐徐下）

第四幕

時：唐文宗開成四年冬，距第三幕已二年

景：曲江離宮盧輕鳳寢宮，與第二幕之佈置略有不同。

人：盧輕鳳、盧飛鸞、彩玉、來喜、李商隱、楊賢妃、殷公公、羽林軍多人。

幕啓時：

是冬天的季節，冷颼颼的感覺。配音效風聲，輕鳳獨自一人，在鼓著錦瑟，幕後女聲哀怨的低聲吟唱著：「相見時難別亦難，東風無力百花殘，春蠶到死絲方盡，臘炬成灰淚始乾……」突然弦斷了……歌聲亦嘎然而止。

彩玉拿了件斗篷，自內走出。

彩：娘娘，……天好像要下雪的樣子，……你把斗篷披上吧，……別著涼了。

鳳：（披上斗篷）奇怪，……弦怎麼突然斷了呢？……會不會李公子……今天不來了……不，……他說來，……一定會來的，……會不會出了什麼意外？……最近，……我的左眼，突然老是跳個不停，……難道是什麼不祥之兆？……（彩玉聞腳步聲，去門外察看，回來說）

彩：娘娘，……鸞娘娘來看你了。……

（飛鸞自外進入）

鸞：鳳妹，……我給你服用的藥丸，……吃了以後，……是否舒服些？……有沒有再噁心，要吐的感覺？

鳳：姊，……好多了！……

鸞：鳳妹，……我方才聽宮裡來的人說，……前一陣子，東宮太子自殺死了的那件事，……又有了新的傳說，……他們，說，太子，……還只有十二歲，……不可能因為怕父皇要殺他，……才去上吊自殺的。一定是被人害死後，才裝扮做上吊自殺的。

鳳：嗯，……這說得也有道理，……他整天只知道和那些樂官，女倡，混在一起玩，不想讀書是真的，怎麼會因為皇上，突然把那些樂官女倡都殺了，……就害怕得自己去上吊自殺呢？……這似乎說不通。

鸞：大家都在說，……準又是那蛇蠍美人楊賢妃，在背後耍的把戲。……你記不記得？四年前，王德妃也是這樣莫明其妙地氣死的，……王德妃死了以後，她就整天在皇上面前說東宮太子的壞話，……說他只知道玩耍，不肯用功讀書，……將來怎麼能繼承皇位，要皇上，……廢了他太子的名位，……後來是因為一些老臣的竭力反對，……才沒有成功。

鳳：姊，你是說，……楊賢妃因為自己沒有生育，……所以，她要想法子，把東宮太子給害死！……好再立那位母事於她的安王溶，繼任太子。……

鸞：對了，……不過，她是個聰明人，……她決不會自己動手，……去做這件事，留下什麼把柄給人

　　逮到！……鳳妹，……你真得小心提防她一點，……因為你曾為皇上，生了個皇子，……如今，

……她下一個要剷除的目標，……可能就是你呀！

鳳：（驚駭地）姊……你別嚇壞了我，……我的兒子，……才不想繼承什麼王位呢？……

鸞：鳳妹，……俗話說，「害人之心不可有，防人之心不可無」，……為了保護你自身的安全，……

逃避楊賢妃的加害，……你還是理智一點，……拔劍斬了情絲，和李公子，早點了斷，別再糾纏

交往下去了！……

鳳：姊，……你要我和他……做個了斷？……

鸞：鳳妹，……你若再這樣痴迷下去，……遲早，會出亂子的！……你別以為楊賢妃在宮裡，整天和

皇上在一起，……而你在離宮的事，……她就一點也不知道？……你錯了，……離宮這兒，她都佈了

不少眼線，……你的一舉一動，……她都清清楚楚，……李義山，……那一天來和你相會，……

自然會有人向她報告，……一旦事機成熟，……她來個活捉，……你就死路一條了！……

鳳：姊，……你說得太可怕了，……我又沒和她爭風吃醋，……楊賢妃她自己背着皇上也有情人，她不

可能來離宮害我的！……

鸞：鳳妹，……姊是一片好心，……才和你這樣說。……當今朝廷上，明分為牛、李二黨，……這你

清楚嗎？

鳳：以牛僧孺一派為首的叫「牛黨」，以李德裕一派為首的叫「李黨」，這些，我還不知道嗎？

鸞：過去李公子，……在令狐楚的與元幕府做巡官，是「牛黨」中的人，最近，令狐楚死了，他卻又投入王茂元的幕府，去做起校書郎來，……變成「李黨」中的人，……像他那樣朝秦暮楚，變來變去的人，……絕非是一衷情至義之士，……你對他是真心誠意，……他對你，卻是虛情假意，……我勸你，睜大眼睛看清楚……還是趁早把他忘了的好。

鳳：姊，……義山，對我絕非虛情假意，……他有他的理想和抱負，……他跟我說過，……他不願被捲入朋黨之爭的漩渦中，……他是超然的……只是爲朝廷做事。

鸞：鳳妹，方才我聽到一個對你很不利的消息，……你想不想知道？

鳳：對我很不利的消息？……姊，……你快說呀！

鸞：有人說，……李義山，好像已經做了王茂元節度使的東床快婿，和王家的二小姐，成親了。……

鳳：（強烈配音）他……已經成親了？（傷心哭了起來）

鸞：大家說，要不然，他才不會這麼容易的，通過了吏部「博學鴻詞科」的考試，被派出去做一名九品官呢！

鳳：他和我說過，這一次完全是憑他自己的本事，通過考試才去做官的！……難道是他故意在騙我嗎？……

鸞：不，……我不相信。……

鸞：鳳妹……你是在離宮，……外面什麼消息都不知道，……所以，被矇在鼓裡。……聽姊的話，……把眼淚擦了，……別再和他交往了。……

鳳：姊，……我……不能和他斷！……斷不了！……

鸞：為什麼斷不了呢？……

鳳：彩玉……你到外面去看看，……李公子……他來了沒有？……來的話，……先來通報一聲。

彩玉：是，娘娘，……（退下）

鳳：（支開彩玉後才說）姊，……我和你實說了吧！……我已經懷了他的孩子！

（音樂又強烈的升起）

鸞：什麼？……你懷了他的孩子？……真是他的骨肉？……

鳳：皇上，已經很久沒……臨幸我了，……除了他，……還會有誰呢？……

鸞：（想起）難怪，你說，這一陣子，老是噁心，想吐，……又老想吃酸的東西！……害我還專誠替你帶胃藥來！……

鳳：兩個月……還不到。……

鸞：現在幾個月了？……

鳳：姊，……你說，……我該怎麼辦？……

鸞：（察看其肚子）現在，還看不出來，……但是，……遲早會看出來的，……這……怎麼辦呢？……

……

鳳：姊，……我想回皇宮去，……想法子主動去親近皇上，……

鸞：不，……那樣，……更糟！……（想了一下）眼前，……只有一條路可走。……吃……打胎的藥，……

鳳：姊，……讓它人不知鬼不覺的流掉，……

鸞：輕鳳，……你可不能一錯再錯了！……為了保住你自己的性命，……你就非這樣做不可！……否則，……誰也救不了你。……

鳳：這是我的骨肉，……我不想這樣做！……

鳳：真只有這一條路可走嗎？……

鸞：（自外進入）娘娘，李公子，他來了。……

彩：輕鳳，……你暫時，先去房裡避一避，……讓我來和李公子談，……看他有什麼辦法，……來收拾這樣的殘局！……

鸞：彩玉，……你陪娘娘進去，……

彩：娘娘，……我們進去吧！……

（鳳無奈的，和彩玉進入後房，不久，李商隱，仍換穿內侍服，進入）

商：大姐，……您好，……輕鳳呢？……

鸞：她病了，……剛才，……在這兒吐了一地，……現在在房裡休息，……我去請了御醫，……一會兒就來了。……

商：是不受了風寒？……還是吃了不乾淨的食物。……

鸞：李公子，……你去門外守著，若有人進來，先咳嗽一聲。……

彩：是，……鸞娘娘。（退下）

鸞：李公子，……我聽說你已經通過了「博學鴻詞科」的考試，派到了官職，做了九品官，我得先向你道喜啊！……

商：大姐，……只不過是個小小的校書郎而已。……

鸞：這比你過去，在令狐楚與元幕府，做巡官總強多了，……對了，……我還聽說王茂元節度使，非常賞識你的才華，……你幫他寫了不少的章奏，他很高興，已經把他的二小姐，許配給你，你做了他的東床快婿，……是真的嗎？

商：大姐，……王茂元節度使，很賞識我，是真的，……他也真有意將二女許配於我，……請了好幾個人與我正式提親，……但是，……因為我心中已有了輕鳳，所以，我一直拖延著，沒有正式答應。……

鸞：聽你這麼說，……你對我妹妹的感情，完全是真心的囉！……那你打算什麼時候？……正式娶我的妹妹過門呢？……

商：我……是有這樣的打算，……只是我眼前的處境，……還有困難！……

鸞：李公子，……有一件事，……我必須要告訴你，……你和我妹妹，相識已經有四年了，……我也相信你，……不是個負心的人，……但是，你們這樣沒有婚姻關係的私下交往，……性命都隨時會有危險。你知道嗎？……現在，……我告訴你一個很重要的消息，……我妹妹，……她已經懷

商：了你的骨肉，……你說，你究竟有什麼打算？……還準備繼續拖下去嗎？……

鸞：（如雷轟頂）什麼？……輕鳳，她……已經有「喜」了？……

商：這些日子，皇上已經有很長一段日子，未來到她宮裡臨幸了，……一旦，發覺她有了喜，……不但她自己性命難保，……恐怕，你也逃不了宮中律法的制裁！……

鸞：輕鳳，她也不知道該怎麼辦？……禍是你闖的，……你總不能不認賬吧？……

商：我……絕對認賬，……我願負起我的責任！……

鸞：李公子，……你能負什麼責任？……你敢親自去跟皇上說，孩子是你的，……要殺就殺你，讓輕鳳不要死，……孩子也不要死！……你真要敢這樣去說，……皇上也不會就聽你的，……讓輕鳳還活在這個世界上。……

商：大姐，……依你說，……你有什麼好辦法沒有？

鸞：我是想了個辦法，……可是，輕鳳，她不肯這樣做！

商：什麼辦法？

鸞：我要輕鳳，吃打胎的藥，……讓孩子流產！……可是，她不同意。

商：不，……大姐，……我也不同意！……我不希望，……這個骨肉，還沒有來到這世界，……就結束了生命！

鸞：哼，……你還真和輕鳳，一個鼻孔出氣。……那我問你，……你要這孩子生下來，是不是？……

你不怕連累到，……你和輕鳳，都會有性命的危險！

商：為了愛輕鳳，……愛我們的孩子，……我願意和輕鳳，要生，就生在一起，死，……也死在一塊

兒！……我甘心。

鸞：（感動）……你，……為了輕鳳，……真的一點兒也不怕死？……

商：（堅定的點頭）嗯！

（輕鳳自臥室激動地衝出）

鳳：商隱，……你這樣說，……太使我感動了，……真情可以感動天地，……我希望老天爺可憐我們，……

讓我們能找到活路。……可以活下去。

商：（沉思）……對，……我們，……好好的來想一想，……能不能找到一條活路？……

鸞：我不相信，……除了我的辦法，……還有更好的活路？

商：（來回躑躅了一陣）啊，……我突然想到了一個好辦法。……

鳳：商隱，什麼好辦法？……快說呀！

商：我過去在玉陽山學道的時候，認識一些道士，我去拜託他們，先找妥一家收留女道士的道觀。……

你再去請求皇上，准你出家修道，到道觀去做女道士，這樣，你不就可以安全出宮了嗎？……

等出了宮，……我們再想法子，另找房子，……把孩子平安的生下來，……

鳳：啊，……商隱，還是你聰明，能想出，這樣好的辦法，……只是，皇上，……會准我去出家修道

嗎？……

鸞：鳳妹，你早就是被打入冷宮的嬪妃，……我想，只要你有決心，……皇上也許會批准你去出

家修道的！……可以試一試。

商：輕鳳，……為了我們的未來，……我們要小心保密，……絕不能洩露半點風聲。

鸞：嗯，……李公子，為了安全為了不洩密，……以後，離宮，你最好少來，避免節外生枝。……

商：大姐說得很對，輕鳳，……以後，我們不能再常見面了。……

鳳：商隱，可是，……我會日夜想著你，念著你！……

商：（想起，自身邊拿出一個玉盤）輕鳳，……我帶了一個玉盤來送給你，剛才一打岔，差一點忘了，……

你看，這上面刻了我的名字，……還刻了一首我寫的詩。……（將玉盤交給輕鳳）

鳳：（看玉盤，唸上面的詩）「雲母屏風燭影深，長河漸落曉星沉，嫦娥應悔偷靈藥，碧海青天夜夜

心」……商隱，你怎麼會想起寫這樣的詩句：「嫦娥應悔偷靈藥，碧海青天夜夜心……」……

……

商：你忘了，前兩天我們二人在曲江邊賞月的情景，……我指著天上說，天上有一個月亮，水面也有

一個月亮，……兩相對映，多美。……你淘氣的故意丟一個石子，到水裡去，……結果水裡的月

亮，就打碎了。……為了表示我倆心中的月亮，永遠不碎，……所以，我特別送這個玉盤給你，

鳳：……你看，它圓圓的，不跟天上的明月一樣嗎？……

商隱……你眞是一個十足的詩人，……做什麼，……都充滿了詩意，……我會珍藏這份禮物，……看見它，……就等於看見了你。……（說著把玉盤放在梳桌上。）

（彩玉自外匆匆進入，小黃門來喜隨後上）

彩：娘娘，……不好了，……來喜說，……有重要的事，向你稟報。……

喜：啓稟鳳娘娘，鸞娘娘，……我看見楊賢妃娘娘，……突然帶了一大批羽林軍從皇宮趕到離宮來，說是要搜查謀殺東宮太子的元兇，……好像是沖著鳳娘娘來的，……特提早來報信，……希望娘娘，……能有所準備。……我走了。（說完即行禮離去，下）

鳳：什麼？……楊賢妃……從宮中帶了羽林軍來抓我？……

鸞：鳳妹，……我要你小心提防，沒說錯吧！……李公子，……你快走吧，……讓羽林軍逮住，……你就見不到明天的太陽了。

鳳：彩玉，快護送李公子出去，……走邊門，……

彩：娘娘，……我知道。

商：輕鳳（依依不捨）你……小心，……應付。

鸞：鳳妹，……別難捨難分的，……讓李公子，快逃命要緊！……走吧！

（二人這才黯然分別，彩玉帶商隱自邊門逃逸，下）

鸞：鳳妹，……你快去房裡清理一下，……把李公子寫給你的那些信，還有那些「無題」的情詩，都

鳳：是，姊，……我這就去清理。（入內屋下）

鸞：（把桌子上的玉盤藏起來，放入一桌子抽屜內）

殷：（人未上場前，先在門外大聲吆喝著）各位軍士注意，寢宮前後左右，嚴密看守，沒有楊娘娘的

（不多一會兒，楊賢妃，由殷公公陪同，率領了一批羽林軍，自外進入，羽林軍四人，站在門外。）

命令，任何人都不准放行，……聽清楚了沒有？

（眾軍士齊聲回答：「聽清楚了。」）

殷：（大聲）楊賢妃娘娘駕到。……

（一陣腳步聲，四下散開。殷公公才進入寢宮，）

鳳：楊娘娘，吉祥。

鸞：楊娘娘，吉祥。

楊：（進入）免禮，……起來。……（殷找座位讓楊坐下）

鳳：楊娘娘，這麼冷的天，……從宮裡趕到離宮來，……是否有重要的吩咐？

楊：（故作輕鬆）啊呀，……輕鳳，……是皇上的旨意，……要我來的，……說是離宮裡有些妃嬪、

點火燒了吧！……遲了讓搜出來，……可就麻煩大了。

鸞：（輕鳳、飛鸞，上前跪迎）

婕妤、才人，……因為得不到皇上的寵愛，私下偷情幽會，有違宮闈視聽，……特命我來清查一下，……輕鳳，飛鸞，……若有冒犯之處，還請勿怪罪於我才好唷！……

鸞：楊娘娘，宮闈門禁森嚴，……那會有這樣的事？……

楊：門禁森嚴是不錯，不過，也有可能被買通了，百密一疏。……（向外發令叫）軍士們，……進來，給我徹底的好好搜一搜！……

（羽林軍四人，進入上場：……）

羽林軍：是。（四人分作四個方向，進入內展開搜查。）

楊：若是發現什麼男人的扇子、手帕、衣帽等用物，……一律呈上來，向我稟報。……

羽林軍：是。（一人吩咐其餘三人，欲進屋時，楊又將之叫住）

楊：慢著，……一定要仔細搜查，……什麼書信、文字，……或是紀念信物，……也不得輕易放過。

（羽林軍四人，進入上場：「是」）

（輕鳳神情緊張、鸞打岔企圖解圍）

楊：楊娘娘，……這是莫須有的傳言，……皇上怎麼會輕易就相信了呢？

楊：（皮笑肉不笑）自從東宮太子自殺身亡以後，傳言可多著呢？……都說我是背後的元兇，……飛鸞，輕鳳，你們說，可怕不可怕？……幸好皇上信得過我，……要不然，……我早就被打入冷宮，……

……或是被送上了西天了呢！……

羽林軍：（先後上場）啟稟楊娘娘，⋯⋯並未搜到可疑之物。⋯⋯

殷：啟稟娘娘，⋯⋯外面下雪了。⋯⋯

楊：好極了，⋯⋯通知出去，⋯⋯注意雪地上，有無留下腳印，⋯⋯依循腳印追蹤，⋯⋯務必把可疑之人抓住。⋯⋯

羽甲：是，⋯⋯娘娘，⋯⋯我這就去通知大家。（下）

楊：繼續仔細搜查。

羽乙：是。（二人入內屋檢查，「羽乙在台上檢查，⋯⋯開抽屜⋯⋯忽發現玉盤，呈給楊）

羽乙：啟稟娘娘，⋯⋯這兒有一個玉盤，⋯⋯上面還刻了詩句⋯⋯

楊：（陰沉的笑）輕鳳，⋯⋯這是那兒來的？⋯⋯不會是皇上送給你的吧？

鳳：啟稟娘娘，⋯⋯這，⋯⋯是小時候，⋯⋯家父所送。⋯⋯

楊：飛鸞，⋯⋯是嗎？你是姊姊，⋯⋯你有沒有？⋯⋯

鸞：（急圓謊）是家父所贈，⋯⋯我⋯⋯的那隻，⋯⋯不小心打破了。⋯⋯

楊：（看玉盤上的詩句）⋯⋯「嫦娥應悔偷靈藥，⋯⋯碧海青天夜夜心」，輕鳳，這詩句，也是令尊寫的嗎？

鳳：⋯⋯是⋯⋯我自己寫的！⋯⋯

楊：我不相信，是你寫的？⋯⋯殷公公，天太冷了，⋯⋯你帶路，送我回宮去吧！⋯⋯這個玉盤，⋯⋯

……我會呈上去，……讓皇上……來問個明白！……

殷：是，娘娘。……

（楊先下，殷隨後，羽林軍亦隨之出去，下。）

（舞台靜默一分鐘，人已遠去）

鳳：姊，……（急哭了）怎麼辦？……怎麼辦？

鷥：（擁鳳入懷）鳳妹，別哭！……要來的，……遲早……會來的。

（燈光漸暗下去，暗下去）

（窗外雪花飛著，風聲加強）

（幕徐徐下。）

尾聲

時：同序幕

景：同序幕

人：李商隱、韓畏之、盧輕鳳、盧飛鸞仍是第四幕打扮、彩玉亦同

幕啓時：

仍是序幕時情景，商隱與畏之二人在飲酒對酌。

天上仍飄著雪花。遠處有寒鴉在聒叫著。

商：「夕陽無限好，只是近黃昏」……畏之，……來，為過去乾了這一杯。……

（二人乾杯後，停一會兒……）

韓：商隱，……人在年青的時候，動了眞情，難免會做一些糊塗事，……你也不用太過份自責了。……

還是把剛才說的故事，繼續說下去吧，……後來，……後來，……又怎麼樣了呢？

商：（沉默無語）……此情可待成追憶，只是當時已惘然……

（商默默垂淚，「錦瑟」主題音樂升起，他自牆上取過錦瑟，順手鼓了幾個音，倏然而止，……）

韓：義山，你怎麼啦？……

商：（突然無語）……

韓：義山，後來，又怎麼樣了呢？

商：畏之……（如被驚醒過來）……我剛才，說到那兒啦？

韓：你說到楊賢妃帶了不少御林軍，匆匆來到離宮，……要進行搜查的時候，……你得到消息……先走了一步，……逃了出來，……這時候，天下起雪來。……

商：我現在還記得很清楚，那一天，颳著北風，下著大雪，幸好老天保佑，讓我從水路，平安的逃出了禁宮，保住了性命，……但是，回到家以後，通宵都沒有闔上眼睛，我擔心輕鳳，她會不會被關了起來，被嚴刑拷打。……

韓：若被關起來，一定會被上刑拷打。……

商：我左思右想了一夜，第二天，我決定想找人設法去營救，又想派人去打聽，可是誰能為我去營救？……誰又能為我去打聽？……我獨自一個人徘徊在曲江的江邊，急得如同熱鍋上的螞蟻一般，又像個束手無措的幽靈一樣，……真不知該如何辦才好。……唉！……（頓足撫胸）我頭腦一片空白，竟然一點辦法，也想不出來。……

韓：後來呢？

商：三天以後，我收到輕鳳派人送來的一封信，……還有，就是這一具錦瑟……（他撫摩著瑟，如同撫摩輕鳳一般）……我會鼓瑟，也是她教我學會的！……這是她留給我唯一的紀念品。……

韓：那封信上，她怎麼說？

商：她……（泣不成聲）

韓：她被抓了起來，才寫的？

商：不！還沒有被抓，她就寫了！……

韓：然後呢？

商：然後……

韓：她被皇上……賜死了？……

商：（鄭重否認）不……她為了怕連累到我，……還沒被抓起來，怕受刑逼供，……就先跳井而死了！……

韓：……

（音樂升起）

商：她給我的那封信，是跳井以前寫的絕命書，……她說怕被拷問時受刑不過，把我招了出來，……才決定先自盡的。送信來的人說，她死了以後，她姐姐也跟著跳進了景陽井，……隨她一起，同赴黃泉，……從此，我再也見不到她倆姐妹的影子了！……

韓：什麼？……她是先跳井而死的？……

（沉默半響，受感動而拭去眼淚）商隱，……我記得，你成親的那一天，臉上一點笑容也沒有，……我一再的問你，還有什麼不開心，不滿意的？……你就是閉口不說，……這個啞謎……隔了這麼多年，……你才給我揭開，讓我明白究竟。……

商：畏之，……這是我一生中，……最令我心碎的一件往事，……也是一椿我最不想讓人知道的心底
　　秘密，……沒想到，……今天多喝了幾杯，……就糊裡糊塗的給你說了出來！……唉，……想收，也
　　收不回了。……

韓：義山……放心，……我向你保證，決不會隨便去和人說，……尤其是，……在我內人面前，絕對
　　會為你保守這個秘密。……

商：賤內走了，……希望她地下有知，……也能原諒我當年的苦衷。……

韓：（看天色）呀，起風了，……說不定，一會兒就飄起鵝毛雪來了，……我得告辭回家去了，……
　　你身體不好，……也別喝了，早點去休息吧！

商：畏之，……（仍有醉意的）別走，……酒逢知己千杯少，……你再陪我，好好喝幾杯！（又再斟
　　酒）

韓：義山，改天再喝吧，……我走了，……再見。

　　（韓起立，商送韓出門離去）

商：醉了也好，一醉解千愁！

　　（他獨自倒酒來喝，燈光漸暗至全黑）

　　（台上燈再亮時，可安排一個替身，穿他的服裝，趴在桌子上，睡著了，發出鼾聲）

　　（夢境的音樂升起，在昏暗的燈光配合下，商隱在趴睡著的人背後站立起來，……顯示他是在做

尾　聲

一〇五

夢，那個人仍在睡著）

（有敲門的聲音，他走去開門）

商：誰？……誰在敲門？……

鳳：是我！……你還記得我嗎？……義山，……

商：（驚喜地）什麼？……是輕鳳？

（商開門，輕鳳在乾冰製成的輕霧中出現，依然當年的服裝）

商：（揉了揉眼睛）輕鳳，……真的是你嗎？……

鳳：義山，……你……把我忘了？……

商：鳳！……（上前，二人相擁抱在一起）……我日夜思念的鳳……你終於來看我了！……

鳳：義山，……你怎麼變得這麼蒼老了……差一點，我都不認得你了。

（二人鬆開）

商：鳳？……

鳳：是嗎？……我們分別已廿多年了，……時間過得好快！……鳳，……這些年，……你有沒有思念，想著我？

鳳：義山，……你說，……我會不想你嗎？……你忘了你寫給我的詩句……「嫦娥應悔偷靈藥，碧海青天夜夜心」……

商：（迷惑地）輕鳳……我是不是……在做夢？……怎麼還會和你見面呢？

鳳：義山，⋯⋯人生本來，⋯⋯就是一場夢！⋯⋯記得當年，我們相識的時候，⋯⋯就像是在做夢。

⋯⋯那時候，你好年青，爲了想擠入士林，不斷用功參加科舉考試，⋯⋯抱著滿腔的熱情，希望

能爲國家盡一份心力，⋯⋯可是受了朋黨的猜忌傾軋，⋯⋯在宦海中浮沉了廿多年，你究竟又得

到了些什麼呢？⋯⋯

商：輕鳳，⋯⋯你說的對，⋯⋯究竟得到了些什麼呢？⋯⋯

鳳：義山，⋯⋯自從你妻子過世以後，⋯⋯前幾年，⋯⋯你一個人在川東，孤零零的，⋯⋯下著雪的

冬天，也沒有人來爲你縫一床禦寒的棉被，⋯⋯長夜孤枕獨眠，⋯⋯精神苦悶到了極點，你的上

司柳仲郢，好意賞你一個歌妓，讓你調劑一下生活，⋯⋯你卻一口回絕了，這又是爲了什麼？

⋯⋯

商：輕鳳，⋯⋯我怕雪，⋯⋯每當下雪的時候，⋯⋯我就想起廿多年前，⋯⋯我離開你，逃走的情景，⋯⋯

⋯⋯你所給我的這份眞情，⋯⋯是我這一生，永遠難以忘懷的，⋯⋯唉，⋯⋯此情可待成追憶，⋯⋯

⋯⋯只是當時已惘然！⋯⋯

鳳：義山，⋯⋯我留給你的錦瑟，你還常玩嗎？

商：我怕鼓瑟，⋯⋯那，⋯⋯就會想起你。⋯⋯輕鳳，⋯⋯一切俱往矣，⋯⋯過去，我害怕被捲入朋

黨之爭，⋯⋯害怕，楊賢妃知道了我倆的秘密，⋯⋯如今，楊賢妃也死了，連皇上，也都已換了

好幾個，現在，⋯⋯你完全自由了，⋯⋯我們可以不管一切，逍遙自在的生活在一起，⋯⋯你來

鳳：了，……就留下，陪著我，再也別走了，好嗎？（拉鳳入懷）

鳳：（依偎在義山懷裡）義山，……你還是像當年那樣的想著我？離不開我？

商：輕鳳，……誰也不能再把我們分開了。……

（突然，乾冰中帶來了彩玉）

彩：娘娘，……你怎麼耽這麼久，不，不走了呢？……楊娘娘帶著羽林軍追來抓你了。……

鳳：不，……我不走！……我再也不離開義山了……

鳳：姊……何苦一定要我回去呢！……

鸞：鳳妹，……走吧，……回去吧！……再不回去，又有麻煩了……

（彩玉拉鳳，鳳捨不得走，拉扯間，飛鸞來了）

商：輕鳳，……你絕不能走！……

鸞：李公子！他也快「來」了，……你們很快……可以天天在一起了。……

鳳：（追出門去）輕鳳……輕鳳（O、S）聲漸遠去。

商：（鸞及彩合力將鳳拉走了）

（遠處傳來雞叫聲）

（燈光漸亮，顯示曙光照來，屋內漸大明）

（趴著睡的李商隱醒來，他揉著惺忪的睡眼，喃喃自語）

商：輕鳳……怎麼來了，又走了？……剛才……我只是做了一場夢？……

（幕後響起瑟聲，鼓出「錦瑟」的主題曲）

（幕徐徐下。）

尾　聲

（全劇終）

（八十一年十一月十六日初稿）

（八十二年四月十五日三次修訂）

（八十四年三月九日四次修訂）

（八十四年三月廿三日五次修訂）

（八十四年八月十四日六次修訂）

本劇寫作參考書目

舊唐書：文苑傳──李商隱

新唐書：文藝傳──李商隱

玉谿生詩箋注：清・馮浩注　台灣中華書局

樊南文集詳注：清・馮浩注　台灣中華書局

樊南文集補編：清・錢振倫、錢振常注　台灣中華書局

李義山詩集：朱鶴齡箋註　台灣學生書店

中國文學家故事：姜濤主編　莊嚴出版社

玉谿詩謎正續合編：蘇雪林著　台灣商務印書館

新校資治通鑑注：楊家駱主編　世界書局

李商隱評傳：劉維崇著　黎明文化事業公司

李商隱詩研究論文集：中山大學中文學會主編　天工書局

李商隱詩研究：黃盛雄著　文史哲出版社

李商隱和他的詩：朱偰等著　學生書局

李商隱研究：吳調公著　明文書局

李商隱傳：董明鈞著　國際文化事業有限公司

李商隱詩選：陳永正選注　遠流出版社

晚唐傑出的詩人李商隱：郁賢皓　單篇

中國歷代大詩人：綜合出版社

唐史：章群著　華岡出版有限公司

詩詞曲賞析：張夢機等編著　空中大學教科書

歷代社會風俗事物考：尙秉和著　商務印書館

道壇作法：峨嵋居士　逸群圖書公司

道門子弟早晚誦課：峨嵋居士　逸群圖書公司

晚唐風韻：葛兆光、戴燕著　漢欣文化公司

李商隱艷情詩之謎：白冠雲著　明文書局

鳳尾香羅：高陽著　聯經出版公司

十大太監：祁平等著　世界文物出版社

本劇寫作參考書目

「李商隱之戀」四幕舞台劇

李商隱：張淑瓊編　地球出版社

李商隱評傳：楊柳等　木鐸出版社

姜龍昭舞台劇劇本

復　　　　活（獨幕劇）三十八年演出。

寶　島　之　聲（獨幕劇）三十九年演出。

視　　察　　員（獨幕劇）三十九年獲中華文藝獎金委員會獎金並演出。

烽　火　戀　歌（歌舞劇）四十一年由總政治部出版。

榕樹下的黃昏（兒童劇）四十一年獲臺灣省教育廳徵求兒童劇首獎。

奔　向　自　由（獨幕劇）四十二年獲總政治部軍中文藝獎第三名，並由總政戰部出版。

國軍進行曲（五幕劇）四十三年獲總政治部軍中文藝獎多幕劇佳作獎。

父　　與　　子（獨幕劇）五十六年獲「伯康戲劇獎」獨幕劇第四名，並由僑聯出版社出版。

孤　　星　　淚（四幕劇）五十七年獲「伯康戲劇獎」多幕劇首獎，並由僑聯出版社出版，後又改名
　　　　　　　　為「長情萬縷」拍成電影。

　　　　　　「多少思念多少淚」由遠大文化出版公司出版。曾由中央電影公司改編

紅　寶　石（獨幕劇）六十年中國戲劇藝術中心出版。

眼　　（四幕劇）六十四年獲「李聖質戲劇獎」首獎，並由商務印書館出版。

吐魯番風雲（五幕劇）六十五年獲「臺北市話劇學會」第三屆藝光獎，並由商務印書館出版。

金　蘋　果（兒童劇）六十七年獲教育部徵求兒童劇首獎，並由中國戲劇藝術中心出版。

國　　魂（五幕劇）七十年獲教育部徵求舞台劇首獎，七十一年又獲政治作戰部頒發「光華獎」，由遠大文化公司出版。

沒有舌頭的女人（四幕劇）七十一年由遠大文化司出版。

金色的陽光（四幕劇）七十二年獲行政院文建會徵求舞台劇首獎，七十三年並由文建會出版。

幾番連漪幾番情（三幕劇）七十二年受文建會邀請與人聯合編寫，七十三年由文建會出版。

一隻古瓶（四幕劇）七十三年由「文學思潮」雜誌社出版。

孟母教子（四幕劇）七十三年完成，七十七年二次修正。

母親的淚（五幕劇）七十三年獲教育部徵求舞台劇本文藝創作獎第三名，並由教育部出版。

淚水的沉思（四幕劇）七十四年完成，七十七年定稿，獲教育部徵求舞台劇文藝創作獎佳作，並由教育部出版。八十年由文史哲出版社出版英譯單行本。

陶匠與泥土（四幕劇）七十八年完成。

飛機失事以後（三幕劇）八十年完成。八十一年由文史哲出版社出版英譯單行本。

泣血煙花（三幕劇）七十九年完成。八十一年由文史哲出版社出版英譯單行本。

李商隱之戀（四幕劇）八十一年完成初稿，八十四年由文史哲出版社出版英譯單行本。

姜龍昭歷年得獎紀錄

1. 四十一年編寫兒童劇「榕樹下的黃昏」獲臺灣省教育廳徵兒童劇首獎。

2. 四十二年編寫獨幕劇「奔向自由」獲總政治部軍中文藝獎徵獨幕劇第三名。

3. 四十三年編寫多幕劇「國軍進行曲」獲總政治部軍中文藝獎徵多幕劇佳作獎。

4. 四十七年編寫廣播劇「葛籐之戀」獲教育部徵廣播劇佳作獎。

5. 五十一年編寫廣播劇「六六五四號」獲新文藝月刊祝壽徵文獎首獎。

6. 五十三年編寫電視劇「青年魂」獲青年反共救國團徵電視劇佳作獎。

7. 五十四年編寫廣播劇「寒澗圖」獲教育部徵廣播劇佳作獎。

8. 五十六年編寫「碧海青天夜夜心」電視劇獲中國文藝協會頒發「最佳電視編劇文藝獎章」。

9. 五十六年編寫獨幕劇「父與子」獲伯康戲劇獎徵獨幕劇第四名。

10. 五十七年編寫多幕劇「孤星淚」獲伯康戲劇獎徵多幕劇首獎。

11. 五十九年因出版劇本多種，人物刻劃細膩獲教育部頒發戲劇類「文藝獎章」及獎狀。

12. 六　十年製作「春雷」電視連續劇，獲教育部文化局頒「金鐘獎」乙座。

13. 六　十年編寫連續劇「迷夢初醒」，「萬福臨門」節目獲教育部文化局頒「金鐘獎」乙座。

14. 六十一年製作「長白山上」電視連續劇，獲教育部文化局頒「金鐘獎」乙座。

15. 六十一年與人合作編寫「長白山上」電視連續劇，獲中山文化基金會頒發「中山文藝」獎座及獎金。

16. 六十三年製作電視連續劇「青天白日」獲中國電視公司頒發獎狀。

17. 六十四年編寫宗教話劇「眼」獲「李聖質戲劇獎」首獎。

18. 六十四年編寫電影劇本「勇者的路」獲國軍新文藝金像獎徵文電影劇本類佳作獎。

19. 六十五年製作電視節目「法律知識」獲司法行政部頒發獎狀。

20. 六十五年編寫多幕劇「吐魯番風雲」獲臺北市話劇學會頒第三屆「最佳編劇藝光獎」。

21. 六十五年編寫電影劇本「一襲輕紗萬縷情」獲新聞局電影事業發展基金會徵電影劇本佳作獎。

22. 六十五年編寫電影劇本「大海戰」獲國軍新文藝金像獎徵文電影劇本類「銅像獎」。

23. 六十六年製作電視節目「法律知識」獲行政院新聞局頒發「金鐘獎」乙座。

24. 六十七年編寫兒童歌舞劇「金蘋果」獲教育部徵求兒童劇本首獎。

25. 六十八年編寫電影劇本「鐵甲雄獅」獲新聞局電影事業發展基金會徵求電影劇本優等獎。

26. 六十九年獲臺灣省文藝作家學會頒發第三屆「中興文藝獎章」電視編劇獎。

27. 七　十年編寫舞臺劇「國魂」獲教育部徵求舞臺劇第二名，頒發獎狀及獎牌。

28. 七十年編寫電影故事「鳥棚中的奮鬥」及「吾愛吾師」獲新聞局電影事業發展基金會入選獎。

29. 七十一年製作電視節目「大時代的故事」獲中央黨部頒發「華夏」二等獎章及獎狀。

30. 七十一年獲國軍新文藝輔導委員會頒發「光華獎」獎狀。

31. 七十二年編寫舞臺劇「金色的陽光」獲文建委會徵求舞臺劇本第二名頒發獎金及獎牌。

32. 七十二年參加教育部委託中華日報舉辦家庭休閒活動徵文獲第三名。

33. 七十二年編寫電影故事「老陳與小柱子」獲新聞局電影事業發展基金會入選獎。

34. 七十三年編寫舞臺劇「母親的淚」獲教育部徵舞臺劇第三名，頒發獎狀及獎金。廳徵兒童劇首獎。

35. 七十四年編寫廣播劇「江爺爺」獲中華民國編劇學會頒發最佳編劇「魁星獎」。

36. 七十五年力行實踐績效特優獲「革命實踐研究院」院長蔣經國頒發獎狀。

37. 七十七年編寫舞臺劇「淚水的沈思」獲教育部徵舞臺劇本獎頒發獎牌及獎金。

38. 七十八年編寫廣播劇「地下英雄」獲行政院新聞局舉辦國家建設徵文獎獎金。

39. 七十八年編寫廣播劇「血洗天安門」獲警備總部青溪新文藝學會頒發「金環獎」。

40. 七十九年編寫電影劇本「死囚的新生」獲法務部電影劇本徵文首獎頒發獎金。

41. 七十九年編寫電影劇本「綠島小夜曲」獲法務部電影劇本徵文首獎頒發獎金。

42. 八十年製作「大地有愛」電化教材獲中央黨部考核紀律委員會頒發獎狀。

43. 八十二年因服務廣電界三十年獲新聞局頒獎牌一面。

44. 八十二年因屆臨退休獲中國電視公司頒獎牌一面。

45. 八十二年編寫舞臺劇本「李商隱」獲教育部徵求舞臺劇本頒發獎金獎牌。

46. 八十二年編寫廣播劇「李商隱之戀」獲中華民國編劇學會頒「魁星獎」乙座。

THE POET'S STORY

An Original Play

by

Chiang Lung Chao

Translated into English

by

Elizabeth Chiang Moxon

John Sawyer Moxon, Editor

December, 1995

The Liberal Arts Press

P. O. Box 7-99, TAIPEI, TAIWAN
REPUBLIC OF CHINA

Table of Contents

<u>Lee Shang-yin</u>

(811 - 858 AD)

One of the most famous and admired poets in China. His literary name was Yee-san and he lived during the latter part of the Tang Dynasty (618-907 AD). His poems made him immortal and for more than one thousand years people have recited, studied, and memorized his work. Like many artists, ill fate visited him with poverty, loss of love, and other hopeless tragedies which tormented and destroyed him at an early age. Fortunately, in the literary sense, that period of torment and suffering was the time that produced his best work. His works move your heart and soul, because you can almost feel his pain. One can't help but wonder whether the immortality of his works was worth the suffering. It is a subject worth a fuller debate.

Lee's father died young, and, with the children's help and hard work, his widowed mother raised and kept together the family of seven. At a very young age, he showed signs of being a promising scholar. Lord Nien took him under his wing, giving him a job at the age of eighteen, in order to support his family. Lee and Lord Nien's son Nien Who-tow grew up together. They were the best of childhood friends, playing and studying together. People around Lee especially respected his gift for poetry.

In spite of his genius, creative talents, and hard work, he had difficulty passing the official exam for a government post. In China, throughout history, until the end of the Chin Dynasty in 1911, other than bribery or nepotism, the only way for scholars to gain government posts was by taking a government examination. The higher the score, the higher the job ranking. The time that Lee was taking the exam and seeking a government appointment, was one of the darkest periods in China history.

Because of the ignorance and poor health of the Emperor, his eunuch meddled in politics, and the resulting conflict with the existing cabinet officials caused widespread bloodshed. Supported by the military, the leader of the Eunuch Party, Chou Shih-liang openly took bribes for fixing official business. The opposition party led by Prime Minister Lee Xuen did plenty of political maneuvering on their own, resulting in a government in chaos.

Lee had neither a prestigious social economic background nor was he interested in nepotism. Lee was, however, famous for his poetry, and was eventually appointed to an official government position. He was however caught between two opposing political parties, one led by his mentor and

former patron Lord Nien and his son, and the other led by his father-in-law, who respected Lee's talent enough to overlook his social background and take him as a son in law.

Although Lee tried to stay out of the political conflicts, both parties wanted him to be on their side. He was torn by his past and present obligations. Eventually both parties denounced him and accused him of betrayal. It was worse than death for an honest and dignified artist to get caught in such a brutal political crossfire. Researchers have speculated that the tragedy of his love affair, combined with the emotional drain of his political career, caused his early death at forty-seven.

Given the painful circumstances, Lee produced the most beautiful poems although with much sadness, frustration, and helplessness. His poetry, read by millions through time, has made his work classic and him immortal. Readers can feel his emotions, and, as you are reading, you can't help but feel a lump in your throat and tears in your eyes. Often, his love poems lack titles, and have vague subjects and much ambiguity. For centuries many of his poems have remained mysterious puzzles.

In recent years, after decades of intensive research, scholars have come up with a theory which may indicate why his poems were so evasive. Apparently he had a love affair with the Emperor's concubine. In China, The Emperor was regarded as a son of heaven. Commoners were not even allowed to look at him. A crime of this magnitude at that time, was punishable not only by death for him but also for his whole clan as well. He expressed his hopeless love and passion for her in his poetry and kept it vague enough to protect his family. Thus developed his timeless style of writing. This is a play which depicts that interlude which left him with a broken heart but a treasury of wonderful poetry.

Time: 835 - 858 AD.

Prelude: 858 AD. A snowy winter night.

Act 1: 835 AD. Fall. Twenty-three years earlier.

Act 2: Ten days later.

Act 3: Next year, 837 AD, late spring, early summer.

Act 4: Two years later, 838 AD, winter.

Act 5: Continued from prelude, 858 AD, winter.

Place: Zhen Zhou (Lee's humble home)
       Chang An (Lee's residence in capital city)
       Qu Jiang (Emperor's summer palace city)

Scenery:

1: (Prelude, Act 1 and Act 5) Lee's humble home in the country (Zhen
    Zhou). A modest hut surrounded by bamboo fence. For the
    Prelude and Fifth Act: snowy winter nights. For the First Act, a
    winter afternoon but not snowing. Center stage is the living room.
    Walls on both sides, up front on the right next to the wall are trees,
    and flowers. Left wall is the main entrance where people enter and
    exit. Bedrooms and kitchen are at back. Table and chairs for simple
    living, eating, and drinking. A long desk for studying and playing
    harp.

2: (Act 2) Bedroom chamber in Palace (Chang An). Center stage is sitting
    area, right side leads to a bedroom. On center stage, there are a
    table and chairs for the monks to sit and pray. On the table, there
    are candles, an incense burner, and various items for the monks to
    use. There is another long desk for the harp. The scene is in the
    palace. Heavy curtains, lanterns, large columns and hallways in the
    background show opulence.

3: (Act 3) Lee's house in Chang An, capital of that period. It is his official
    residence. It is equipped with better furniture, compared to the first
    hut. Scrolls hang on the wall, high back chairs, candlesticks and a
    bookcase. It is tastefully decorated for a scholar's residence. Left

3

side of the stage is the main entrance, Right side leads to other rooms.

4: (Act 4) Resort palace: A room in a resort palace. From the windows the view of the mountain and lake. Outside, there are winding walkways and lanterns. It is a dressing room, with bureau and dressing table. You can see palace guards in the distance.

Characters:

Lee: The poet, Act 1 to 4, young dashing scholar in his twenties. Full of energy and in his glory when in love. In Prelude and Act 5, he is in his forties, looks depressed and in poor health. By old Chinese custom, other than to your elder, it is not polite to call a person's name to their face. Usually they address each other by their literary name. You will see Lee being addressed as Yee-san, rather than Shan-Yin at times.

Han: Lee's good friend, his literary name is Wei Zhi; later becomes his brother in law. A young man from a rich family, dressed in expensive clothes. In the prelude and last scene he and Lee although are the same age, but appear strongly contrasted in looks, attitude, and spirit.

Mom: Lee's mother, a widow in her forties, motherly warm and sweet, trying to look after the whole family.

Ching-yu: Lee's younger brother in his early teens.

Nien: Son of Lee's patron, a noble man. Lee's childhood friend. The son of a high ranking official, opulent dress.

Liu: A Taoist monk. He is Lee's teacher, when Lee goes to the temple in the mountains to learn the truth about life and nature.

Phoenix: The Emperor's concubine. A beautiful young lady in her twenties, who loves literature and music. She should have the air of a princess and be very sophisticated.

Argus: Phoenix's older sister, also one of the Emperor's concubines. A smart, calm and elegant lady.

Jade: Phoenix's maid, 17 or 18 years old, smart and cute.

4

Young: Has a Princess title, higher ranking among Emperor's wives. She has a pretty face but an evil mind and expression. She is very shrewd but with poor health.

Ien: A eunuch, who is Princess Young's loyal servant, in his forties.

Merry: Phoenix's young servant, a gofer.

General Lee: A high ranking official. Appears in military casual clothing, with a beard. A warm and sincere elder.

Captain Tien: Secret police type in a special force, in charge of catching dissidents.

Soldiers: (Two, A and B) Act as special forces searching for dissidents. .

Palace Guards: (4 in military uniform). milder looking compared to the soldiers.

Servants: Two Middle aged males, work in Nien's household. Use same personnel for soldiers, and servants to play palace guards. They don't appear at the same time.

Prelude

Time: 858 AD. A snowy winter night

Scenery: Lee's original home, the humble hut.

Characters: Lee is 47 years old with white hair. He looks depressed and in poor health. Han is the same age as Lee, but in good spirits, a strong contrast to Lee.

When the curtain goes up, Lee and Han are sitting facing each other in center stage at a table eating and drinking together. As the lights come on, Lee puts down his wine cup, starts to play his harp and sings a sad tune. (Background music starts).

Lee: (Reciting a poem) "I wonder why my inlaid harp has fifty strings, each with its flower-like fret an interval of youth... The sage Chuang-tzu is day-dreaming, bewitched by butterflies, The spring-heart of Emperor Wang is crying in a cuckoo, Mermen weep their pearly tears down a moon-green sea, Blue fields are breathing their jade to the sun... And a moment that ought to have lasted for ever has come and gone before I knew....."[1]

(Why does my inlaid harp have fifty strings? Each string and each fret remind me of glorious days. Sage Zhuang Z is infatuated by butterflies in his day- dreams. Emperor Wang sent his yearning through the crying of cuckoos. Mermen weep their pearly tears into a moon reflected deep sea. Blue fields warmed up by the sun, evaporate the jade from ground into thin air. All our passion was gone before I could grasp it.)[2]

Han: Yee-san, what's wrong? What's bothering you? come on, there is plenty of food and wine. Tonight is a good time to talk about the past.....

[1] Three Hundred Poems of the Tang Dynasty 618-906. An English Translation v. Chinese Text. Witter Bynner. Tung Hai Book Co., Taichung, Taiwan, 1967.

[2] as translated by Elizabeth Moxon.

Lee: (sinking in his thoughts) God, time flew by so fast. With a blink of our eyes, twenty some years have gone by. Do you remember when we first met? We were so young... dashing... now... my hair is white, and I feel old.

Han: Don't talk about being old. You are only forty-seven, what's the matter with you?

Lee: You and I passed the official test the same year. However my career was rocky, my family life was not harmony like yours... Ai... The last twenty years I went through hell... It's too much. I can't stand it any more.

Han: Listen to you, you sound old and too depressing. As I recall, when you were young you went to Yu young mountain to study Taoism. Now you are studying Ch'an in Buddhism. You should be the one to enlighten, and figure out everything in life.

Lee: Yes, I did. Because of that, I realized that I have sinned... Especially when I was young... Something I did... It has always haunted me. The pain in my heart.

Han: If so, how come I didn't know anything about it? You and I are best friends and also in-laws, why didn't you tell me?

Lee: Ai...What can I say? Somethings you just can't ... let's drink.

Han: Let's drink, bottoms up. Have some more. It might help you to get it off your chest.

Lee: I am sure that I'll feel better if I talk about it. However, you have to keep it a secret, promise me that you won't tell...

Han: Of course, you have my word. (Music gradually starts while the lights start to dim. Lee starts to tell the story which leads to Act one.)

Lee: That year... I was 24, I left and decided to study to take that year's official exam. At the same time, a bloody struggle started in the government. The Gan Lu massacre... It started as Prime Minister Lee Xuen attempted to stop the eunuch's corruption. The eunuch leader found out and counterattacked the Prime Minister's party. No one with even a remote connection was spared. Family members slaughtered by the hundreds. (the noise of metal swords clashing, people screaming, crying......)

ACT ONE

Time: 835 AD. 23 years before the Prelude.

Scenery: Lee's original house. A modest hut.

Characters: Lee at twenty four. Mom, Han in twenties too. Ching-yu, Nien, Monk Liu, two servants who work for Nien, Army Captain Tain, and two soldiers.

As Lee is telling the story in the prelude (stage hands change the scenery to Act 1) After the fighting and killing gradually fades, the curtains go up. On stage is Lee's humble home, before he obtains any official post. It is a winter afternoon but not snowing. Lee's mom is sweeping, cleaning the table and tidying up the room. Yu rushes in from outside, closes the door, huffing and puffing.

Mom: Ching-yu, you are a bit early today.

Yu: Mom... big trouble, Master Hu's family is in trouble.

Mom: What happened? Tell me!

Yu: The soldiers from the special force took their son, and confiscated their property. They said that Master Hu was friendly with the Prime Minister. He was accused of treason by Chou Shih-liang, the head of the Eunuch Party and has already been executed. Now for security reasons, they are going to kill all the traitor's offspring too, in order to prevent future revenge.

Mom: Oh, my God! Master Hu was such a kind person; how could this happen to him? I can't believe that he would do anything bad. Oh dear....we are going to have a hard time. When there is no justice, there is chaos.....

8

Yu: Yes, Mom.... I also heard that Chou Shih-liang, you know... the leader of the Eunuchs was so mad that he was killing everyone in sight. They said the massacre victims included toddlers......Some of them knew what was ahead so they committed suicide ...... Chou is still throwing their bodies into the river ......

Mom: Oh! My God, this is horrible... How did our Emperor allow this to happen?

Yu: People on the street said that since the Emperor had a stroke a couple of years ago, he doesn't do much any more. The Eunuchs waited on him, kept him happy, and alienated him from the outside. Official business was conducted by bribing them first. Under the name of protecting the Emperor's health, they guard him like a prisoner. No one can say or do anything without them knowing first.

Mom: This is awful. Ching-yu, It's chaos outside, you better stay put, you hear?

Yu: Yes, Mom...

Mom: By the way, where are your brothers?

Yu: Number two and number three brothers are still at work. Shang-yin is at Master Chen's copying books for them.

Mom: Good. The only one that I am worrying about is your brother Shang-yin. He loves to criticize the system and the government. I know he resents those crooked Eunuchs. I pray that no one will report him to get him into trouble.......

Yu: Mom, don't worry. He is not an official, and we have no money. No one will notice him... (A series of knocks on the door; Mom and son both get nervous.)

Mom: I wonder who is out there.

Yu: (nervously walks toward the door) Who is it?

Han: (from outside) It's me! Is your oldest brother home?

Mom: (Relaxed) Oh! It's Mr. Han, come on in.   (Motions Ching-yu to open the door)

Han: (Walks in; greets Mom) How are you Mom? Is Yee-san home?

Mom: No, he is not home yet; he should be home soon. Ching-yu, go get your brother. (Mom pours a cup of tea for Han)

Yu: Yes Mom, I'll be right back!

Mom: Have some tea; he will be here soon.

Han: Thank you Maam! I didn't mean to bother you. I am here to bring Yee-san some news.

Mom: News? I hope it's good; can you share it with me?

Han: Yes Maam. I am concerned about him. With his talent, we all know that he should have no problem with the official exam. The last two times, he didn't make it, and I found out why. Apparently you have to bribe the testing official to pass. Also there is another way to get in. That is to join a fraternity group and ask the leader of the pack to smooth the testing official for you.

Mom: Oh! I see.

Han: Last year the number one scholar, do you know how he got his high marks?

Mom: No, I don't. How did he?

Han: I just heard recently, that he used Eunuch Cho's connection. He was given the highest mark because the price was right.

Mom: I can't believe they even got into the official examination fields.

Han: Of course, that is the beginning of all lucrative posts. Actually, they will bully into anything as long as you give them what they want.

Mom: In that case, we might as well forget about the tests.

Han: No! don't give up. That is why I am here. Accidentally I found out that the person who is in charge of the testing is a good friend of the Niens. The senior Nien is Yee-san's mentor and the junior Nien is Yee-san's best friend. All Yee-san has to do is ask the Niens to put in a good word for him. That way he will be done with the test.

Mom: Is that all?

Han: Yes, if Yee-san will ask, I can guarantee....... The only thing is....
   Knowing him and his personality, I am afraid that he won't do it.

Mom: When he comes back, I'll talk to him.....This is the most important
   thing in his life....

Han: Yes, I know. Oh! there is another thing I want to mention to you.
   Please tell Yee-san to be careful. At least for the moment, not to
   write those satire poems. The Eunuchs have spies all over the
   place. They are killing innocent people daily. I want to make sure
   that he doesn't get into trouble by writing any more sarcastic
   poems.

Mom: What do you mean? Did he write any thing that was not appropriate?
   I don't know anything about it.

Han: In the last two weeks, many good families who have any connection
   to the Prime Minister were killed by the Eunuch gang. Some were
   honest high ranking loyal officials. Yee-san was outraged by the
   brutality. He wrote two poems voicing his anger. I am afraid if they
   fell into the wrong hands......

Mom: Oh my God! How could he do this! I don't know where he put it, I
   hope he burned it.

Han: When he showed it to me the other day, I ripped it up right a way. I
   don't know whether he showed it to any one else or not, that's why
   I want to warn you.....

Mom: Ai, I have to speak to him about this. He is too honest and too
   straightforward for his own good...... (Lee walks in along with
   Ching-yu)

Lee: Hi Mom, and how are you Wei Zhi (Han's literary name)? I am sorry to
   keep you waiting.

Mom: Mr. Han was concerned about the two poems that you wrote. Where
   did you put them? Please show me.

Lee: Mom... Why? You rarely read my poems.

Mom: Stop talking, just get it for me.

Lee: (goes to the bookcase finds the draft and hands it to Mom)   Here
    they are.

Mom reads it with horror on her face and rips the paper into pieces.

Lee: Mom, what are you doing? That's my work.

Mom: I know that's your work. I just want to save your life. I know it makes
    you feel good to express your feelings, but I don't want to lose you.
    Don't you ever use your head?

Lee: I am sorry, I was angry at what's happening.

Han: We know that. At this moment, no one is safe; we are worried about
    you.

Lee: Are you really that concerned about the poems?

Han: Yes. We are best friends... I know you, and understand how you feel.
    I know your temperament, if the poems fell into their hands, no one
    can save you.

Lee: I know that, It's my work, I take full responsibility.

Mom: (Angrily) That's enough! We know how you are, that's why he is
    here and I ripped up the paper.

Han: Now, now. I am sorry, I caused all this, I better go now. I'll come back
    some other time.

Mom: Thank you Mr. Han, I am grateful for everything.

Lee: Yes, thank you my friend. I'll see you soon. (Lee sees Han off and
    closes the door)

Mom: Shang-yin, come over and sit down, I want to talk to you.

Lee: Yes Mom.

Mom: Mr. Han told me that he found out that the person in charge of the
    government testing is good friend of the Niens. All you have to do
    is to ask the Niens to put in a good word for you.

Lee: No, Mom... There is no way that I'll do any such thing. Because the Niens were good to me, more reason for me not to do it. No, no, absolutely no.

Mom: Other people all do it. You are brilliant, we don't ask much, only to put a good word in......

Lee: I don't care what other people do. I will not do it.

Mom: Can't you just give it a try? They all know how bright you are. They all admire you, they will not feel any different about you if you ask.

Lee: Mom, stop... Let's drop the subject. If I do this, no matter how successful I am in the future, I'll never feel good about myself. So the answer is no.

Mom: Ai, we knew you are going to be like this. If you continue to be so stubborn, you are going to miss out on a lot in life. (the sound of people pounding on the door from outside).

Tian: Open the door! Hurry up!

Lee goes to open the door, one captain and two soldiers come in.

Lee: What can I do for you?

Tien: I have special orders to search every house for suspects and suspicious activities. Go in there and search (Motions the soldiers to go to the back rooms)

Mom: Dear captain, I am a widow, we are in poverty, there is nothing worth searching for here......

Tien: Cut it out! We are with the special force, we have to carry out orders.

Both soldiers come out and report to Tien.

Soldier A: Captain, I can't find anything; there is no one in there.

Tien: Are you sure?

A: Yes, I searched thoroughly.

Tien: (Turns to the other solider B) How about you? Did you find anything?

Soldier B: No, I checked all the furniture, there is nothing there that can hide anyone.

Tien: (Turns to the family) What is your last name?

Lee: Our last name is Lee.

Tien: Good! You are who I am looking for. Who are you?

Lee: My name is Sang-yin, I am also called Yee-san.

Tien: I am sure that you have heard about the traitor Lee Xuen who tried to overthrow our movement. Although he is dead, we are still looking for his allies. What is your connection with him?

Lee: Other than we have the same last name, there is no connection. I have never even met this person.

Tien: We are looking for a monk named Zheng-mi. Is he hiding here.

Lee: If he is a monk, why are you pursuing him?

Tien: He was involved in the plotting. He committed treason. He must die.

Lee: The rebel leader has already died. Monks devote their lives to preaching, he is harmless. Why don't you just take it easy and let it go.

Tien: (Sarcastically) Well! Listen to you, how nice, we should all take it easy.......(Notices pieces of paper on the floor, picks them up and tries to put them together. (Nastily) What is this?

Mom: That's nothing! The kids were scribbling words on the paper, it was for fun. It's no good, you see, that's why they ripped it up. I am sorry that I have not swept the floor yet. Ching-yu hurry, clean it up.
(Ching-yu takes a broom and starts to sweep, Mom tries to get the paper from Tien, but he won't budge.)

Tien: These words are suspicious, sounds like rebel propaganda. This also could be that monk's handwriting. If you tell me his whereabouts, I'll be easy on you.

Lee: You already searched here, why don't you try somewhere else....

Mom: We really don't know anything.

14

Tien: I promise we'll continue searching; however, if the monk didn't write it, who did?

Yu: I did. I tried to write a poem, I couldn't get it right, so I ripped it up.

Tien: You did! All right, you write it again to show me your handwriting.....

Yu: En....(He hesitates)

Lee: Ching-yu, nice try, thank you. Captain, I wrote that, I was depressed so I wrote something to relieve my frustration... But it is ripped.

Tien: Good! you confessed. Come, arrest him. Take him back for interrogation.

Soldier A: Yes, Captain. (soldiers grab Lee and start to move toward the door).

Mom: No, Captain, please don't... I beg you... He didn't do anything.

Tien: (Pushes Mom away) Get away old woman.

(Ching-yu holds on to his mother, someone knocks on the door.)

Mom: Ching-yu, hurry, see who is there. (Ching-yu rushes to open the door. In come two well-dressed servants, loaded with gifts).

Servants: We are here to see Mr. Lee.

Yu: (Excitedly turns toward Mom) Mom, the young Mr. Lien is here. (Lee frees himself from the soldiers and goes to greet Lien. Tien and the soldiers are surprised by the new arrivals, they just stand there and watch them).

Lee: Oh, my dear friend, it's so good to see you.

(Lien walks in, greets Lee and Mom; he appears surprised by the soldiers.)

Lien: How are you Maam? Yee-san, is everything all right? What's going on here?

Mom: Oh, thank goodness you are here. We have some misunderstanding here with this captain. I am so glad that you are here.

Lien: What kind of misunderstanding?

Lee: Let me introduce you to Captain Tian, he is in charge of the special force to clean up the rebels. This is my mentor General Lien's second son the honorable Mr. Lien who is now the special adviser to the Emperor. Captain by any chance do you know each other?

Tien: I have always admired your father, the General, for a long time. I am sorry that I have never had the honor to meet you.

Lien: The pleasure is mine. After I left the capital, on my way here, I heard about how hard you all have been working. My childhood buddy here must have done something wrong to cause the misunderstanding. Please accept my apology.....

Tien: Oh, no, no, there is no need. I am only doing my job. Well, I guess I ought to search somewhere else. Pardon me, we have to leave now. (All three exit).

Lien: Yee-san, what did happen?

Lee: I was so disgusted by what's going on in the government, I wrote some poems. It almost caused me some grief.

Lien: I know how you are. Unfortunately the devils are in power now, you better curb yourself.

Mom: Thank you for saving him. I am also grateful for all these gifts ... you are too generous.

Lien: Please don't mention it. My father wanted me to bring these over. It gives him great pleasure to see you all enjoy it.

Mom: Please give him our best regards. How is he? In good health, I hope?

Lien: Thank you, he is fine. He is looking forward to seeing you all. He asked me to hand deliver a letter. Father is getting old and really needs Yee-san's help. He hopes that you will leave things here behind and go to work for him. (Gets out a letter and hands it to Sang-yin to read).

Mom: Thank you. Sang-yin still won't give up, he wants to try the exams again. After he passes, then he'll go. He just wants to prove that

16

he can do it. I heard that you are friendly with the person who is in charge.......

Lee: Mom, please stay out of this, don't interfere.

Lien: Yee-san, if you want, I'll be happy to.

Lee: No, please don't. I want to do it on my own.

Lien: Yes, I respect your feelings. What about my father's request? Are you going to assist him or not.

Lee: I would love to work for him, but it has to wait until next spring after the exams. If I pass, it will make any appointment legitimate rather than personal.

Lien: All right, I'll tell him that. By the way, have you been to Yu Young mountain lately?

Lee: No, not lately. Why? Are you interested in Taoism?

Lien: No, I just remember what you told me before; how majestic that Yu Young mountain is. You were marvelling about those temples. I figure the weather is perfect and I have few free days, maybe you and I could take a trip to visit those temples.

Lee: I have not thought about those temples for a long time.

Lien: Really? what happened to your lady friend, that Taoist nun?

Lee: Oh, Her... Forget about her. We lost contact a long time ago.

Lien: That's too bad.

Lee: As the saying goes : nothing lasts forever. Long lasting love is very rare. If it's meant to be, you will run into it. But if you go out looking for it, you will never find it.

Lien: Gee....Sounds like you are not in the mood to accompany me for some fun......

Lee: I am sorry, I have a lot on my mind. Maybe some other time.

Lien: All right! It's getting late, I have other things too. I'll see you later.

17

Mom: Won't you stay for dinner? I'll get some food and wine so that you two can celebrate and catch up.

Lien: No, thank you, maybe another day. I'll be back.

Mom: You do that. Make sure we have a chance to treat you for a decent meal.

Lee: Let me walk out with you.

(Lee exits to say good by, Mom checks the gifts with Ching-yu. When Lee comes on stage again, Mom motions to both of them.).

Mom: Come on, you both help me to move these gifts to the back. (While the three of them are working some one outside at the door is knocking and asking)

Liu: Yee-san, Are you home?

(Ching-yu rushes to the door lets Liu in and goes to call Lee.)

Yu: Brother, Master Liu is here to see you.

Mom: Welcome, Master Liu, Ching-yu hurry up; pour some tea.

Lee: (Rushes over and bows to Liu) Master, It has been a while, how are you?

Liu: I am fine. I have been thinking about you. I am passing through, so, I stopped to see how you were doing.

Mom: Have some tea, and I'll leave you two talking. Quien-u, come help me. (Mom and Ching-yu exit).

Lee: Master, what have you been up to recently?

Liu: I have left Yu Young mountain, travelled a bit. Do you know that recently the Palace needs monks to help with funerals?

Lee: With the number of people that have been killed, I am not surprised that they have a lot of funerals.

Liu: No, this is different. You are talking about the massacre following the failed coup attempt on those Eunuchs. I am talking about the death in the Emperor's family.

18

Lee: I am confused. I don't know what are you talking about.

Liu: A few days ago, the future Queen, Princess Wong died.

Lee: You mean the Eunuch murdered the future Queen?

Liu: No, the rumor said it has something to do with the Emperor's favorite concubine, Princess Young.

Lee: Indeed, this is news to me.

Liu: The deceased Princess is our Crown Prince's mother. Out of respect, the Emperor is giving her a full royal burial. They are setting up religious rituals to release the souls from suffering. I think the Emperor wants to do something for those who died innocently to ease his guilt.

Lee: I think the most unfair thing in the world is that the Emperors are surrounded by hundreds of women. From Queen, to princess to concubine, all they do is to please him. Their only hope is to produce the Crown Prince. The magnitude of the power struggle due to jealousy is incredible.

Liu: Those poor women. I heard stories, that some girls were sent into palace at the age of fourteen. Throughout their whole lives, if they are lucky they may exchange a few words with the Emperor. Few are adored by him. Most spend their whole lives in waiting.

Lee: This is not just sad, it is cruel......

Liu: I am a monk, I better not talk about woman too much. Let's get back to the subject. I remember once you told me that when the opportunity arose, you would like to see inside the palace. Now is your chance.

Lee: What do you mean? (While they are talking Ching-yu quietly comes in and listens to them)

Liu: Because of the need for a large number of monks, I don't think they will be too picky on the qualification of the monks. Although you are no longer in a temple studying, you know what to do from the past. Let me take you along, so you will get some new experience.

19

Lee: This sounds great, I hope we can fool them and not cause you any trouble.

Liu: I know we will be fine. You were and still are my best disciple. You are brilliant with the religion and know the procedure. Put on the rope and the hat, you are more qualified than anyone I know.

Lee: Listening to you, I am excited. This is the chance of a lifetime. How often does one have a chance to see inside a palace. My only concern is that I might lose some study time for the exams ...... (Mom comes in from back)

Mom: My son, I am still worried about that Captain Tien. He still has those pieces of paper. What if he comes back? It might not be a bad idea for you to go with Master Liu for a while until things calm down a bit.

Lee: (Thought about it) Yes, you are right, Mom.

Yu: (Quietly motions to Lee) I want to go too.

Lee: You too? (Motions him to talk to Liu).

Yu: Master Liu, May I join you too? I can dress up as the young monk disciple. Although I don't know much, I can be a gofer. I am good at helping with odds and ends. I promise I'll be careful.

Liu: (looking at Yu, nodding his head) All right, I'll take you along as a helper to move equipment and set things up. Do you think you can handle it?

Yu: Yes, I can. Thank you! Mom, is this all right with you?

Mom: Only if you promise to listen to Master Liu. Make sure you are careful in the palace.

Yu: (Excited, clapping his hands, jumping up and down) Great! Thank you Mom. I am going to tell the others. (On his way out, he is so excited, he trips and falls, gets up and continues running)

Lee: Careful! Gee, look at him (Every one laughs. Lights out. Curtain down).

Act 2

Time: Ten days later.

Scene: Inside the Palace, Lady Phoenix's bedroom chamber, sitting area.

Characters: Phoenix, Argus, Jade, Merry, Princess Young, Ien, Lee, Ching-yu, Monk Liu.

Curtains up, Phoenix sitting at a wide but shallow desk alone, playing the harp. The music is sad, light smoke slowly rises out of the incense burner. When the music is about to end, Jade walks in.

Jade: My lady, you can stop for a while now, you have company, Lady Argus is here to see you. (Phoenix stops, gets up and walks over to greet Argus)

Phoenix: Oh, dear Argus, I have been waiting for you.

Argus: I know.... I heard that you have trouble sleeping.....I asked the doctor to fix you a special remedy. He said for you to take some of this, before bed time. It should relax you and give you a good rest. (Takes out a bottle and hands it to her).

Phoenix: Thanks, dear sister. (She takes a look at the bottle then hands it to Jade) Jade, put it on the table next to my bed. (Jade walks toward the bedroom and goes in).

Argus: Dear sister, have you heard any rumors about the cause of Princess Wong's sudden death?

Phoenix: Yes, Jade told me that the rumor was that Princess Wong did not die of a natural cause. It is more likely that she was poisoned by someone.

Argus: Yes. That is what I had heard too. (Jade comes out from the bedroom) Jade, you go to guard the front door, if someone is coming, let us know first.

Jade: Yes, my Lady. (Jade leaves the stage)

Argus: Do you know who did it?

Phoenix: No, I have no idea......

Argus: What I heard was that Princess Young... you know that eunuch servant of hers... he ordered his gofer to do it. The evil princess was behind the plot.

Phoenix: Princess Young! Oh dear, why would she do such a horrible thing?

Argus: They were in competition to gain more attention and favoritism from our Emperor. They were at it for a long time, finally she got a chance to get rid of her.

Phoenix: Our Emperor....does he know?

Argus: Of course not. No one dares to say anything for fear that it would cause more deaths if he gets angry. This is only the rumor. There is no evidence to prove anything. That is why they could get away with it.

Phoenix: Oh, dear, it is frightening.

Argus: That's what I would say. Dear sister, let me warn you. That Princess Young is a snake with such a phony personality. Behind her beautiful smile is a sharp knife, always there waiting for you. Although she comes to see you often, seems friendly and kind to you, don't let her fool you a minute. She is checking on you constantly. You don't really know what she has in mind, especially now that you have produced a son for our Majesty, and she still hasn't. Just think, if your son were selected to be the heir to the throne, then you would be crowned as Empress, and surpass her in ranking. Where will that leave her? There is no way that she will stand still and let it happen. That is what happened to Princess Wong. The way it looks, you may be her next target. You must be alert and careful, you can't afford make any mistakes around her........

Phoenix: Yes....Sister....thank you.

22

Argus: We are blood sisters, although we both belong to one man, I'll never jealous of you. I'll always look after you....

Phoenix: I know, you don't have to say it, I always know.

Argus: Princess Young is cruel and vile, like a poisonous spider, a rare species. She is jealous of everyone in her way, she must get rid of anyone whom the Emperor takes a liking to. If she could, she would kill everyone and have the Emperor all to herself. (Jade runs in and cuts her off).

Jade: My ladies, Ien is leading Princess Young on their way here.

Argus: Speak of the devil... (Ien comes in and bows to wait for Princess Young to come in).

Ien: Your Highness, her Highness Princess Young is here to see you.

Phoenix: Phoenix greetings to Your Highness.

Argus: Argus' greetings to your highness.

Young: Thank you, at ease.

Phoenix: Jade, bring our best tea to Her Highness and guests. (Young sits down, Ien stands behind her, Jade goes off and later brings in the tea).

Young: I am here to see you and to extend a special invitation to my chamber for a drink. I have fresh crabs and newly bloomed chrysanthemum flowers. We could recite poetry, enjoying flowers while we are eating and drinking. We will have a good time together. Argus, I want you to come along too. I have Osmanthus wine for you, I know it is your favorite.

Phoenix: It is so kind of Your Highness, I would love to go, except today there are some monks coming to exorcise to release suffering souls. They should be here soon, I can't leave now.

Young: What happened? Why are you having monks here? Have you run into any ghosts?

Phoenix: I have had trouble sleeping lately. Insomnia really bothers me. After Princess Wong passed away, late at night and early in the

morning, I often hear footsteps. Last night, I even heard a flute playing the saddest tunes.

Young: (nervously) Really?

Phoenix: Princess Wong used to play the flute, it was her favorite hobby. I am afraid that her spirit may be lingering around due to her sudden and unwilling death. Fortunately, the last few days we have had quite a few monks in the Palace to do religious rites for her. I requested a few to come to my chamber too, in order to really let her soul rest in peace.

Young: Phoenix, do you think those monks really have the power to get rid of ghosts?

Phoenix: I guess so; this is their specialty. Otherwise our Emperor wouldn't have them here to do the rituals.

Young: I guess you are right. (Merry comes in bringing Monk Liu with her).

Merry: My lady, the monks are here for the ritual.

Phoenix: Please bring them in.

Liu: In the name of our mighty God, my greetings to my lady. (Monk bows to her).

Phoenix: At ease, this is her highness Princess Young, and Lady Argus....(Lee and his brother come in with a wooden crate; they proceed to take out all the necessary items for the ritual: incense, burner, candles, paper money, a tablecloth and sacrificial fruits, etc.)

Young: Your eminence, my chamber needs you to chant sutra too, will you be free to do it soon?

Liu: Surely, Your Highness, as soon as we can.

Argus: My place too, please.

Liu: Yes, Your Highness. (Turns to Lee) Are you all ready?

Lee: Yes, we are ready to start.

Liu: Good, I'll start now. (Opens the book and starts to chant).

Young: Phoenix, I better go now so that they can do their thing. You, Argus, you come along with me, I want you to keep me company and have drinks with me.

Argus: All right Phoenix, I'll see you later. (Young, Argus and Ien exit).

Liu: Your highness, your bedroom? Are we allowed to go into your sleeping chamber to exorcise around your bed?

Phoenix: I think so, let me take you, this way please. (Phoenix brings the monk and Lee off stage.) (Ching-yu and Jade are the only two left on stage).

Yu: Miss, your mistress, the Princess Phoenix, is she from eastern Zhe Jiang?

Jade: Yes, how did you know?

Yu: My brother and I lived there when we were young. Her accent is familiar to me.

Jade: The man who came with that monk is really your brother?

Yu: Yes, he is the oldest in my family. Lee is our last name. His first name is Shan-yin. mine is Ching-yu. What is the princess' name?

Jade: Her last name is Lu, and first name is feathery Phoenix. She was chosen to be one of our Emperor's concubines. She is beautiful and talented with many things. We call her Princess Phoenix.

Yu: Yes, Miss. What is your name? and how should I address you?

Jade: My name is Jade. My family name is Shen. I am the lady in waiting, you may call me Jade.

Yu: Jade...It is a beautiful name.....(looks around and walks toward the inlaid harp) What is this? Does the princess play this?

Jade: This is called a Spinet, it is a beautifully inlaid harp. When you flick the strings, it creates pleasant sounds. When you learn how to play it well, it makes beautiful melodies. Originally it had fifty strings, but it has now evolved into different versions, some are twenty-five, some are twenty-three and some are only nineteen.

Yu: Gee, you are quite knowledgeable.

Jade: I learned a great deal from the Princess, she is so smart, she is kind and... (Jade stops when Liu, Lee, and Phoenix come on stage).

Liu: Your Highness, I am finished here for the moment, the rest of the procedure, Lee will take care of and finish up for me. I think your chamber will be fine from now on. If you hear anything at night again, I'll come back again to clear it for you. Please excuse me, I should go and check the other parts of the Palace to make sure their rituals are going as well too.

Phoenix: Surely, thank you for everything.

Liu: Shang-yin, later, add more incense, recite more charms and sutras. I'll see you later.

Lee: Yes, I'll follow the instructions......Ching-yu, prepare the incense. (Liu exits).

Yu: Yes! (Starts to prepare the necessary items for the ritual.

(Lee performs the Taoist ritual and helps the Princess bow and kowtow etc. When it is over, while Lee is picking up his things, he turns toward the Princess.)

Lee: Your Highness, all the exorcise rituals are done, I ask to be excused now.

Phoenix: Just a moment, can you wait a few minutes?

Lee: Yes, Your Highness, what may I help you with?

Phoenix: I would like you to draw a couple of efficacious charms on paper to place on my doors. Then the ghosts won't enter my chamber. Isn't that the way you normally do it?

Lee: Efficacious charm? Oh... Just a minute .... (signals Yu to come over).

Phoenix: What happened? Did you forget the ink and brush? Jade, go to my desk and bring out the writing tools.

Lee: Oh, not just that, I also forgot the special sacred paper. Ching-yu Please go find our teacher, and ask him to draw two Efficacious charms on sacred paper for the Princess. Hurry back!

Yu: Yes, right away. (Yu hurries off stage, and Jade comes out with the writing tools on a tray).

Phoenix: Mister, I have been observing you. From your performance, you don't really look professional. You even forgot the paper, the most important part of the ritual. Who are you? What kind of phony game are you playing? Tell me the truth, otherwise...

Lee: I... I... I was Reverend Lieu's student... I.... I am not phony.

Phoenix: You are still denying it. All right, Jade, call the security guards.. (As Jade leaves, Lee stops her).

Lee: Please don't. As long as the Princess spotted me, I have no choice but tell you the truth. I am a poor scholar. I am in the capital here for the high ranking exam. I am in need of some living expenses. My former teacher brought me here to help him, to earn a day's wage. I truly was the reverend's student for a while. I am not deliberately trying to deceive you, Princess. Unfortunately Your Highness is too bright for me to get away with it. I am very sorry.

Phoenix: Oh!... an educated scholar. In that case, I won't be difficult. Can you show me how well you can write?

Lee: Princess you still sound suspicious of me. In that case, I can no longer be humble, I have to prove to Your Highness. (Lee picks up the brush, thinks a while and starts to write, while they all watch. Lee finishes, and hands it over to the Princess) Your Highness, please feel free to express your opinion.

Phoenix: (reading out loud) New sprout covered with husk freshly from forest, price high as gold in town. At where gourmet abundant, who could deprive new growth of young! (When finished, she turns to Lee) Mister, please explain.

Lee: This is my opinion of people who dig up bamboo shoots to use for food. What a shame, if people would only let the bamboo shoots have a chance to grow into bushes or a forest, wouldn't it be better?

Phoenix: I see... you are hinting that useful young men aren't given a chance to develop to their fullest, before they are destroyed.

Lee: Your Highness is very intelligent. You understand what I mean.

Phoenix: How old are you, Mister?

Lee: I am twenty-four; I was born in the year of the snake.

Phoenix: You were! What month then?

Lee: The fifth of March.

Phoenix: Yes, I was born in September, the same year. How many brothers and sisters?

Lee: I have four sisters, one died young, and three brothers. The one with me here today is my youngest brother. My name is Shang-yin, and he is Ching-yu.

Phoenix: That's nice. I have no brothers, only a sister. Her name is flying Argus. She is a year older than I am. My name is feathery Phoenix. We used to live in Eastern Zhe Jiang. Ten years ago, we were selected by the local officials and offered to the Emperor. We have not left the palace since.

Lee: Your highness grew up in Eastern Zhe Jiang! No wonder your accent is so familiar and homey.

Phoenix: Is that so? No wonder I... I feel... we... it seems we have met before. I feel like I have known you for a long time. I also love poetry, but I can't write as well as you do. I admire your choice of words. It is perfect.

Lee: When I was sixteen, I impressed the intellectual circle with my two theses. However, eight years have gone by, I still haven't gotten anywhere.

Phoenix: No wonder you are using bamboo shoots as an example. You are still young; don't get discouraged; I believe in your abilities. I know you are going to be somebody someday.

Lee: Thank you for your kindness. If I have Your Highness' luck, I'll be fine.

Phoenix: You think I am fortunate to be here? Yes, everyone thinks living in a palace is wonderful, but no one understands the stifling, lonely and boring life here. Ai! I better not say any more...

Lee: Your Highness, it is harder than ever for ordinary people to get into the Palace. You eat the best food, wear the best clothing, you can have anything you want. You even have the Emperor's love. Why are you still not happy?

Phoenix: Anything I want? How about my freedom? My free will? The Emperor's love? How long does the Emperor love a woman? I can't believe an intelligent person, like you, doesn't see our point of views. Have you ever heard of the poems about the ladies who lived in the Forbidden Palace?

Lee: Yes, I seem to remember. But, Your Highness, those were people who work in the Palace, You are a Princess, it is different.

Phoenix: You are a male, you don't understand... Princess, workers, when you lose your freedom, there are no differences in feelings of pain and suffering.

Lee: I think I understand what you are saying. Life itself actually is more suffering than joy. (Yu comes on stage with some paper in his hands)

Yu: Your Highness, the Efficacious charms are here for you. The Reverend said, one on your door, and one on your bed frame, you should be well protected.

Lee: Ching-yu, give them to me, I'll go and post them for Her Highness.

Yu: Yes, brother. (hands the papers to Lee. Lee rings the bell and recites the sutra while walking toward the bed chamber. Phoenix follows)

(The lights on stage gradually dim to complete darkness).

(The stage lights gradually turn bright, the scenery shows it is a while later, in the evening of the same day. The lanterns have been lit, Phoenix is sitting down and savoring a poem written on a handkerchief).

Phoenix: "The stars of last night and the wind of last night At west of the Painted Chamber and east of Cinnamon Hall. though my body has

no wings like those of the bright-colored phoenix, I still feel the harmonious heart-beat of the Sacred Unicorn." [3]

(Last night's star and last night's wind. Fell in love at the west of the painted chamber and east of cinnamon wing. Have no wings like the colorful Phoenix to fly together. Yet, our hearts are able to feel and echo our passion. like the mythical horn to feel and echo our emotions.)[4]

(Phoenix loves the poem, reads with a light heart, and, at a few places she will highlight or repeat and show that she is moved by the poem) Mmmmmmm........ This is beautiful......(Holds the handkerchief towards her heart with a smile).

(Argus walks into the room quietly. Phoenix doesn't notice.)

Argus: Sister, what are you doing?

Phoenix: (Startled by Argus, instinctively hides the handkerchief) Hi... oh, dear sister... Me?... Nothing.

Argus: What's in your hand? Let me see it.....(while Phoenix resists, Argus playfully grabs).

Phoenix: It's only a handkerchief, what do you want it for?

Argus: (prepares to open the handkerchief and read the poem) Last night's stars and last night's wind... echo our minds. Oh, my goodness, this is beautiful... And look at the handwriting, it is strong and forceful... Sis, this is a love poem, who wrote it?

Phoenix: (Tries to say something, but hesitates). I don't know how to explain...

Argus: Phoenix, are you having an affair? Are you in love with someone?

Phoenix: I...I don't know... I can't tell... It happened so fast, so suddenly... I can't imagine...

[3] Three Hundred Poems of the Tang Dynasty 618-906. An English Translation v. Chinese Text. Witter Bynner. Tung Hai Book Co., Taichung, Taiwan, 1967.

[4] as translated by Elizabeth Moxon.

Argus: Pull yourself together, and tell me what has happened? I am your sister, it's all right to tell me...

Phoenix: Fine, but let me show you another poem of his first. (She goes to a drawer and gets out a piece of paper, hands it to Argus).

Argus: "Eight years old, peek into the mirror, painting the eyebrows long. Ten years old, playing in the field, gathering the flowers to decorate the gown. Twelve years old, learned to play the harp, have not yet stopped. Fourteen years old hide in the deep chamber not ready to wed. At fifteen, quietly weeping under the swing set." This is about us... Who wrote this? How does he know our feelings? Since they forced us into the palace, we have never felt happy enough to have a good laugh. Who is this person? How long have you known him?

Phoenix: Not terribly long... Since the day he came over for the religious rites. He was here to release the suffering souls. Now I am suffering for not being able to release his soul from my heart.

Argus: Yes... I remember... that young handsome one... No wonder, since that day, you've kept saying that the ghosts are still bothering you here and insisted on continuing the ritual... Did he write the poem?

Phoenix: Yes, he did. He wrote quite a few for me, they all beautiful, he is very talented. Unfortunately, the mourning period will be over soon, and there will not be any excuse for him to come here again. I am afraid I won't be able to see him ever in the future.

Argus: I think, it is better that way, for your sake. You must realize your position, you are one of the Emperor's wives, different from a normal girl. You are not allowed to even think about another man, let alone to have an affair; do you understand what kind of risk you are taking?

Phoenix: I know who I am. I am an object, I belong to the Emperor, and I know it is forbidden, but I can't help it. I...I am in such pain. I love him.

Argus: I am glad you know who you are; you have no choice but to forget about him. Don't ask for trouble; he is only a priest, not worthy of your well being.

Phoenix: No, he is not really a priest; he is a scholar with wisdom and quality. In time, he will be somebody extraordinary.

Argus: Forget it! You must forget about him.

Phoenix: I have tried, but I can't.

Argus: You silly thing; what can you do? Even if he became someone special and extraordinary, can he outrank the Emperor? It is impossible. You are surrounded by spies in the palace; you know how cruel it is with the power struggle among the wives. If the gossip reaches the Emperor, I couldn't even save you. Please spare yourself.

Phoenix: I know what you are saying, but I can't get him out of my mind. I can't eat. I can't sleep. I am going out of my mind.

Argus: I think you are crazy to feel this way. You are old enough to understand the consequences. Look at yourself; get a hold of yourself, will you? One wrong move and you will destroy everything. Ai! It is getting late, I am going to bed, you better get some rest too, we'll talk tomorrow.

Phoenix: Yes, I'll see you tomorrow.

(Argus exits; Phoenix looks at the handkerchief, sighs and starts to play the harp sadly. A while later, Jade comes in quietly and walks toward Phoenix)

Jade: Your highness, Master Lee is here to see you.

Phoenix: He is really here? Bring him in. (Phoenix fixes her hair and clothing. Jade brings Lee in to Phoenix. Lee is in different clothing to disguise himself as a member of the palace personnel).

Phoenix: Jade, you guard the door outside for me. If anyone comes this way, signal us by coughing.

Jade: Yes, Princess. (Goes outside).

Lee: I can't believe you play the harp so nicely.

Phoenix: Thank you, but not nearly so nice as your poetry. I should change my name into Colorful Phoenix to fit the one in your poem.

Lee: Princess, the "Colorful Phoenix" in my mind actually is you, the "Light Phoenix". Princess, may I call you by your name?

Phoenix: Of course, from now on, I'll call you by your name too. I love the meaning of Shang-yin, especially the word Yin; it means hermit, invisible. I want you to be invisible to others except me. That way, we don't have to worry about being seen by others, when we spend time together.

Lee: That is why I must see you tonight. The religious ceremonies have come to an end. I am afraid, I'll never have a chance to see you again.

Phoenix: Please don't say that. If you want to, I think we can figure out some way to see each other.

Lee: You think so? Palace security is so tight, even if I had wings it'd still be impossible to sneak in.

Phoenix: I know. Oh, by the way, when Merry brought you in, did you run into any problems?

Lee: No, Merry gave me these clothes to change into, even if we had run into guards, they would have assumed that I work here. I vaguely remember that you have a sweet olive tree in the courtyard; I kind of follow the scent of the sweet olive.

Phoenix: You are so smart... and so different.

Lee: You are smarter than I am. You are the smartest girl I have ever met. You know how to raise silk worms, weave cloth, gather herbs for medicinal use, polish jade, carve horn. The most wonderful thing of all is that you are talented in musical instruments, and understand my poetry.

Phoenix: (Happily) Really? You are too kind. All these things I learned here in the last ten years. It's just a few hobbies, nothing special.

Lee: You are so modest too. You are better than ten talented girls put together. (Holds her gently).

Phoenix: Shang-yin. Have you ever heard of the vacation palace in Chu Jiang?

Lee: No. I don't think so.

Phoenix: Ten miles southeast of Chang An, our capital, there is a resort palace for our Emperor to relax. Every spring, the Emperor brings his favorite wives to spend some time there. The scenery is magnificent. The palace is surrounded by gardens, temples, orchards and lakes. In the spring, thousands of different varieties of flowers bloom at the same time. The color is breath taking; it's like heaven on earth.....

Lee: Yes, now that you mention it, I do remember, every year the Emperor has given the ceremonial banquet there for the top winners of the official exam to celebrate the appointees to new official positions.

Phoenix: That's right. The security there is not as tight, the number of palace guards is less too. It will be easier and safer for us to meet there.

Lee: Oh, that's wonderful; when will you be there?

Phoenix: I told you, we go every spring. Now is only late fall, so at least three more months.

Lee: Three months? That is ninety days. Too long, I can't wait, I wish that you were going tomorrow.

Phoenix: (Laughing) Look at you.

Lee: In the past, other than studies, I didn't do much, life was quite meaningless to me. Now, my life is filled with hope and energy. Every day I look forward to seeing you, and each time we see each other gives me more reasons to live, although those times are too few and far in between.

Phoenix: Yes, myself too. Often I feel like one of the silk worms that I raise. Spinning a silk thread to imprison themselves in a cocoon. There is no meaning and purpose in life to live like that.

Lee: Oh, my sweet lady, don't be depressed like this; even the cocoon finally opens. The continuity of the silk worm is dependent on them to carry.

Phoenix: Do you think we have any hope in our future?

Lee: Yes, I am positive. Look at the beautiful moonlight; even the moon goddess is envious of our love. (They hold and caress each other. Suddenly Jade's cough is heard).

34

Phoenix: For heaven's sake, someone is coming.

Lee: What should I do?

Phoenix: Hurry, go into my bedroom, don't come out until I call you.

(Lee exits stage to back room).

Jade: (Comes on stage from outside, followed by Ien and Princess Young) My lady, Ien has accompanied Princess Young here to see you.

Phoenix: Phoenix welcomes Your Highness (bows to Young).

Young: At ease. (sitting down)

Phoenix: Jade, bring tea for our special guests.

Jade: Yes. (off stage)

Phoenix: Your Highness came at such a late hour. Is there anything that I can do for you?

Young: (Pretending that there is nothing but carefully looking around) Oh, nothing important. The truth is that our Emperor didn't come to me tonight. I have insomnia, so, I came here to find some company, to ease the burden.

Phoenix: (relieved) Oh!...so...

Young: Phoenix....I have a great deal of things on my mind that I want to share with you. May I spend the night here, so that we can have a heart to heart talk?

Phoenix: (Getting nervous) Your Highness, I snore at night. It might interfere with your sleep.

Young: It doesn't matter, I snore too. Ien, you go inside to arrange things and prepare the pillows and coverlets.

Phoenix: Your Highness let me take care of things for you. There is no need to trouble Ien. (Tries to stop Ien).

Ien: (still trying to going in) Thank you, your highness, but it is my duty to serve.

Young: Phoenix, let Ien do it; it's his job.(Uses eye signal to him to go in and search).

(Ien exits off stage, Phoenix is nervous but suddenly gets an idea).

Phoenix: Your Highness...I...I...

Young: Yes, Phoenix what do you want to say?

Phoenix: The truth is that, although the priests have
exorcised my chamber, often in the middle of the night, chilly winds sweep through it. I have even heard sad weeping from time to time. I am getting used to it, but I am more concerned for you. I don't want you to be frightened. You might be better off in your own chamber.

Young: (Half believing but still stalling) Really? What kind of ghosts? Male or female?

Phoenix: Your Highness, I don't know for sure. The ghosts are usually those who died unwillingly and often before their time. Aren't you afraid of ghosts?

Ien: (Comes on stage from inside) Your Highness, every thing is ready for you.

Young: Did you find anything unusual?

Ien: No, I have checked everything, all seems to be in good order.

Young: Phoenix, I think you are right, I better return to my own chamber. I might sleep better there. You get some rest now. Ien, lead the way.

Ien: Yes, Your Highness. (Ien and Young exit).

Phoenix: (Wiping perspiration from her forehead) Gee, that was close!

Lee: (Comes on stage with clothing messed up) It was a close call. Luckily, I was hiding in the closet; it came this close.

Phoenix: Thank God, for sparing us this time. If you were found, that would have been the end for both of us.

Lights out, curtains down, end of Act Two.

Act 3

Time: One year later. Spring and then summer.

Scenery: Lee's house in Chang-An.

Characters: Lee, Mom, Ching-yu, Han, Nien, General Lee, Merry.

When the curtains go up, you see a house near the capital city. The main entrance is located at upper left stage. The right hand side of the stage has a door leading to the inner rooms. The interiors of the rooms are of a higher standard than those of Act 1, due to the owner's position in government. It is still very intellectually oriented, conservative with good taste. From the window, one can see the trees and spring flowers outside in the garden. Inside the room, there are a desk, chairs, bookcase, end tables, etc. Mother is in the room dusting and lightly straightening things. Ching-yu comes on stage in nice decent clothing.

Mom: Ching-yu?

Ching-yu: Yes mother.

Mom: Since we moved here, other than the first few days, you two have not been home much at all. Every day, you leave early and return late. What have you two been doing?

Ching-yu: Mom, it is so exciting in town. There are fancy shops, wonderful restaurants. There is a river called Ch'u Jiang. The scenery is beautiful, and you can row boats on it. There are many magnificent pagodas and gazebos all over the place. The gardens are beyond description; it makes you feel as if you were in heaven. Besides, we were introduced to quite a few new friends. They take turns inviting us for parties because of Shang-yin's new position. We have been drinking, talking, writing poetry and playing games. Life here is definitely better.

Mom: I know, you are young, and you only care about fun things. There are also responsibilities. Since your brother passed the official test,

all of a sudden, people are interested in your brother for marriage. Quite a few matchmakers have sought us out.

Ching-yu: Mom, don't pay attention to those snooty busybodies. They only seek to profit for themselves. They didn't care whether we lived or died before, now they all act like flies circling around you know what, damn opportunists.

Mom: Watch your language. Although you are right, your brother indeed is old enough to get married. For some reason, every time I mention it, he always makes excuses. I can't figure him out; why should he wait...unless he's found someone here in town?

Ching-yu: Mom, you didn't know; he passed the exam; it's a high honor and just the beginning. To qualify for the high rank of a government official, you must pass the hardest exam to be picked by our Emperor.

Mom: Oh...I see...I didn't know. (Lee comes on stage wearing well tailored handsome clothing).

Lee: (Bowing politely) Mother. How are you?

Mom: (Lovingly) Fine, my dear, where have you been?

Lee: I was at General Lee's residence. He invited me for a game of chess. That is why I was late. I am very sorry. (Quietly gives Ching-yu some instructions, following which Ching-yu exits the stage).

Mom: General Lee? You mean The General Lee? Currently the most popular figure in court with our Emperor?

Lee: Yes, mom. He's the one. He lives in a huge mansion. It was given to him by the Emperor. If a person is not careful, he would get lost in there.

Mom: You... socializing with such high ranking officials?

Lee: Yes, mom. Although he is well established, he is a humble man. I respect him for that, and I am grateful that he enjoys talking to me. He wants to introduce me to his circle of friends.

Mom: Oh, that's nice; all his associates are rich, famous and powerful.

(Han comes on stage while mother is talking).

Han: Shang-yin, I am glad that you are home. Mrs. Lee, how are you today?

Mom: Oh, fine thank you, it is so nice to see you. Sit down, I will leave you two to talk. I'll go and finish up some other things. (Mom exits).

Lee: Look at you, you are glowing, what's going on with you to make you look this good?

Han: (Happily) Today I am here on a special mission. I am personally delivering a wedding invitation. I am getting married on the tenth of next month. Since you are one of my best friends, I want to make sure that you will be there. This is the invitation, to honor me, you must come. (Gets out a red envelope and hands it to Lee).

Lee: (excited, happy and loud) What? Getting married? You son of a gun, why didn't you say anything? This is a big surprise, what a shock. Who is the lucky girl? Oh, God she is really lucky to have you as a husband.

Han: She's the oldest daughter of Governor Wong.

Lee: Governor Wong? Oh, Lord, he is the richest and most powerful person in the country. Currently, he is our Emperor's favorite; he can do no wrong. He is willing to entrust you with his number one daughter? You are lucky.

Han: Yee-san, Governor Wong has seven daughters, and, after my wife, he still has six left. You and I are best friends; that's why I am here, to make sure that you will be at the wedding. I want to introduce you to each and every one of the daughters. Take your pick; I'll match you up. I hope we'll be brothers in-law; wouldn't we have fun together?

Lee: Cut it out, stop kidding around. With Governor Wong's wealth and power, he can pick and choose whoever he wants for sons in law. With a modest background like mine, I have no chance. I wouldn't even dream about it. Thank you anyway for your thoughtfulness.

Han: We'll see. By the way, where have you been lately? I missed you quite a few times. When I stopped by General Lee's house the other day, he told me that you and his family went on a trip to Chu-Jiang together. Do you know the connection between General Lee and Governor Wong?

Lee: I thought General Lee mentioned something about being related, but exactly how, is beyond me.

Han: Let me tell you. Mrs. Wong is General Lee's sister, in other words, General Lee is my future wife's uncle.

Lee: Therefore, after you are married, you are not only the son in law of the Governor but also are closely related to General Lee.

Han: Yes, Yee-san. I want to explain a tricky situation here to you. Your mentor and benefactor, Governor Nien, is from a different territory and he is the leader of an opposing party. If eventually you wind up serving under him, we will become political enemies. If that's the case, the chances of us getting together in the future will be slim.

Lee: (Sighing) Ai! A united government could do wonders for its people. Look at it now, our court is divided into two groups, each one is selfishly working for its own interests and at the same time, trying to destroy the opposite party. It is ruining the country and killing a lot of innocent people. Wouldn't it be nice that if we could all work together.

Han: Yes, I agree, but there is nothing we can do. We are the small powerless ones.

Lee: If they continually do this, I am afraid that our Tong Dynasty is going to be shortened. Oh God, I can't even imagine.

Han: Come on, forget it. Let's drop the subject, don't worry yourself sick. It'll all work out eventually. I'd better get going, I have a lot of invitations to deliver. I'll see you at the wedding, all right?

Lee: Of course, I'll be there, good friend. Thank you for thinking of me. (Lee sees Han off stage, turns around and looks at the invitation again with an envious expression) Lucky you, getting married now, God knows when it will be my turn.

(Ching-yu walks in on stage from outside with a letter in his hand)

Ching-yu: Brother, here is a letter for you. Princess said that you must destroy it as soon as you have read it.

(Lee nervously takes the letter, opens and reads it. Phoenix's voice comes from backstage).

40

"My sweet love, our meeting for tomorrow night has to be postponed, due to the fact that the Emperor has decided to entertain some high officials tomorrow night. We were all ordered to be there. I am sorry for the last minute change. I'll try to find a chance to see you soon. Your true love, Phoenix."

Lee: (looking disappointed and hurt, sighs and slowly comes up with a couple of lines of poetry). The time was long before I met her, but is longer since we parted. And the east wind has arisen and a hundred flowers are gone. And the silk-worms of spring will weave until they die. And every night the candles will weep their wicks away.[5]

(Our meetings are hard and our partings are even harder. The East wind had died down, ruined hundreds of blossoms. The silk worms weave silk until they die. The candles shed their tears until they burn out.)[6]

Ching-yu: The messenger specifically said that from now on, you must not take any chances. Some one snitched and Princess Young lectured Princess Phoenix warning her about her behavior. Princess Young said, "By law, for any wrongdoing, the male will be beheaded and the female will be hanged with a silk cord. There is no possibility for mercy, including their families."

Lee: After tomorrow night, they leave and move back to the main Palace. If I don't see her tonight, I probably will never see her again.(Painfully tears up the letter).

Ching-yu: It is too dangerous now. Why don't you just forget about her, and forget about the whole thing.

(Mom walks on stage, finds them talking, stops and listens to them).

Lee: This is impossible. Every minute, day and night, I think about her. How can I just forget?

[5] Three Hundred Poems of the Tang Dynasty 618-906. An English Translation v. Chinese Text. Witter Bynner. Tung Hai Book Co., Taichung, Taiwan, 1967.

[6] as translated by Elizabeth Moxon.

Ching-yu: Well, if that's true, what can you do? Do you think she loves you that much too?

Lee: You don't understand. She loves me. I know she loves me. She loves me so much that we....we have been together. She is willing to give up everything to live a simple life with me for the rest of her life.

Ching-yu: Big brother, you have to understand that she is not a common woman. She is one of Emperor's women. She belongs to the Emperor; do you want to take one of the Emperor's possessions? Are you going to pick a fight with the Emperor? Do you have a death wish?

Lee: No, no, let's figure out something; we'll ask Jade to help. If they can help the princess escape from the palace, we'll run away together. As long as the Emperor can't find us we'll be fine.

Ching-yu: Forget it, forget it, there is no way. It is impossible to find our way around inside the palace, let alone escape from there. Anybody who helped you would have his head cut off. Do you have the heart for that?

Lee: I would rather die than live without her. I'll do it myself. I am going to take a chance tonight. (He walks toward the entrance).

Ching-yu: (Grabs Lee) Stop it; you are crazy; you are going to get yourself killed.

Mom: (Runs out and stands in front of Lee, in a loud voice) Stop it. Shang-Yin, you stay right here. If you don't want to live, how about your mother?

Lee: (Shocked and realizing what is happening, guiltily lowers his head) Mom...I am sorry. Mom, did you hear our conversation?

Mom: I can't believe what I've just heard. I can't imagine that you would fall in love with someone else's concubine. Worst of all, I can't believe that you are willing to risk everyone else's life by doing this. What happened to your upbringing and your moral standards? What happened to your plans for the future?

Lee: Mom, forgive me, this is not easy to explain in simple words. Although she is the Emperor's concubine, she lives a lonely life.

We love each other; why can't I save her from her living hell? Why can't we have a chance to live a free life?

Mom: (Slaps Lee across the face to stop him from continuing) How dare you talk back to me. You are crazy, your are out of your mind. I am ashamed to have a son who fools around with married women. When the Emperor finds out, our whole family will be killed. Have you ever thought about your brothers and sisters' lives? I can't believe you would lose you head over a woman and then cast eternal shame on our family.

Lee: (holding his cheek, showing regret, shamefully kneels down sobbing) I am sorry, Mom.

Lights dim, the stage turns dark.

When the lights go on again, the time has changed to summer. Mother is resting with eyes closed in a chair in the living room; she is waving a fan. Ching-yu is studying at a desk, also waving a fan to chase mosquitoes. Soon you hear the sounds of horses.

Mom: (pointing her fan at Qien-u) Ching-yu, go outside and take a look. It is kind of late to have noble visitors.

Ching-yu: (Opens the door. General Lee enters in casual military uniform but waits at the entrance while Ching-yu rushes over to get Mother) Mom, It is General Lee.

Mom: (Quickly gets up and straightens herself out, rushes to greet the guest) General Lee, please come in, it is such an honor to have you here.

General: Madam, how are you today? Is Shang-Yin home?

Mom: No, I am sorry, he's not, he's at a friend's house. You know, they get together to drink wine and write poetry. He should be home soon. Please sit down. Ching-yu, please pour some tea for General Lee. (Ching-yu brings the tea out and then goes into the back room).

General: Well...all right, I'll wait for few minutes. Thank you. As a matter of fact I want to talk to you first anyway. I am here to propose a marriage.

Mom: Oh! Yes, thank you General. Which family is the lady from?.

43

General: The lady I have in mind is the second daughter of Governor Wong. She also is my niece. This spring Shang-Yin met her at an outing and they even had a chance to talk a little. Apparently they made pretty good impressions on each other.

Mom: Oh, Yes, I remember that Shang-Yin mentioned what an intelligent lady she was. She is a noble lady, but to marry my son; I am afraid we are too humble a family.

General: Oh, you mustn't think like that, Madame, a good marriage is made in heaven, often based on fate. My brother in law told me that he already has every thing that he wants in life. In reality, where can he find a family to match his wealth and power. All he is looking for are good qualities in a young man for his daughters.

Mom: Speaking of quality, I am afraid my son doesn't have it either. When he took the government tests, although he passed the first one, for some reason he did not pass the finals. How can he get anywhere like that?

General: Madame, we all know that our government is very corrupt as to the testing system. Probably, enough people bribed the testing officials that they filled the quota without him on the final list. Whether he passed the test or not really didn't matter to us. The Governor and I both know what an extraordinary man your son is. That is why I am here to propose this marriage.

Mom: Oh! thank you. Since the Governor and you are so kind to honor him, there is nothing I can say but yes. When he comes home I'll tell him. I thank God to have you as my son's friend.

General: As long as you agree, I think Shang-Yin will have no objection. By the way, the Governor's first son-in-law, Master Han is Shang-Yin's long term best friend. If the marriage works out, they will also become in laws. They will be working and drinking together even more often. I think they just might produce some of the best literary work in history.

Mom: Oh, yes. That's right. Now I am positive that Shang-Yin will like this marriage.

General: It's getting late; I won't wait any longer; I am going home now. I am looking forward to the good news. Good night. (The General goes out through the main entrance; Mom sees him off. The noise

of the horse gradually diminishes. Mom comes back to center stage; Ching-yu also comes out from the back room).

Ching-yu: Mom, this is fabulous, no one could ask for a better match. After he becomes the son-in-law of the Governor, all these stupid obstacles will be gone. He will be what he deserves to be.

Mom: You are right. I also think, only after he is married, will he forget the Princess. By the way, has he been sneaking off to meet that woman lately?

Ching-yu: I don't know.

Mom: Are you sure?   You better tell me the truth, before he gets into grave danger.

Ching-yu: I really don't know; he doesn't tell me where he goes any more. I guess he is afraid that I might tell you.

Mom: The way I see it, he is still hung up on that Princess. I bet, he is still risking his life to see her. I must push this marriage; this is the perfect solution. As a matter of fact, the sooner the better.

Ching-yu: Mom, after Shang-Yin gets married, where will I sleep? We don't have any extra space for more people. You are not going to make me sleep in the woodshed, are you?

Mom: We will figure something out. Where are your brothers and sisters?

Ching-yu: Mom, you forgot, they were hired to help with the harvest in a neighboring village. They might not be back until very late.

Mom: That's right, with all the excitement, I forgot all about them.

Ching-yu: Mom, on second thought, maybe we ought to postpone the marriage until Shang-Yin is in a better position to provide a better living for the bride. I don't think that a fancy rich lady would want to live like this. I am afraid she might take a look here and run home crying.

Mom: You are right. I thought about that too! That's why I couldn't say yes firmly. The fancy lady wouldn't want to be a poor family's daughter-in-law. Why should she suffer? Now that I have given it more thought, I can't make up my mind. Yes or no?
(The sound of a carriage outside).

Mom: Go open the door, somebody is here.

(Ching-yu opens the door, Lee comes in appearing drunk. Nien follows him. Ching-yu helps Lee a little).

Nien: Your brother had a bit too much. You better help him to his room.

Lee: (Pushing his brother away) No! Who says I had too much. I am perfectly fine. (He tries to walk in a straight line and can't. Mom walks up to help him).

Mom: Shang-Yin, you've really had too much to drink.

Lee: No, Mom, don't worry, I am not drunk. I was in a good mood, so I let myself go and enjoyed a few.

Mom: All right, in that case, I'll leave you alone. You two sit down then. (Mother off stage to the back room)

Nien: Ching-yu, it's getting late, you better help him. I'm leaving.

Lee: (Grabbing Nien) No! I don't want you to leave yet. I want to talk to you; I have a lot to tell you. I admit that I did have a lot to drink, but people usually express their true feelings only when they have had enough to drink to give them some courage. Don't you want to hear me out?

Nien: Sure, I want to hear you. I won't leave. Go ahead, sit down and tell me all about it. (Both sit down, Ching-yu exits to the back room).

Lee: You've known me since we were about sixteen, right? It was your father who loved my work and helped my family through the hard days. Ever since then, we have studied and played together. The last seven or eight years we've been the best of friends. You should be the one who knows me the best. Tell me, what kind of person am I? Am I one of those politicians who use people or am I one of those greedy merchants who cares only about profits?

Nien: What are you talking about? I know you well enough; there is no question in my mind as to your integrity. Nobody has ever accused you of being that kind of person.

Lee: For my entire life, I have never wanted to hold a high position. I just want to be able to support my family. I hate politics. I hate

politicians. Their friction is ruining our country and tearing the court apart.

Nien: I know; I understand how the current carries us. Sometimes it's out of everybody's control.

Lee: I feel that I was born at the wrong time. I don't want to be dragged into either side of the political arena. I don't want to get swallowed in the whirlpool. Why won't people leave me alone. Can't I have a third option?

Nien: I know that you were treated unfairly when taking the exams. We recognize your quality. My father has always welcomed you to work for him, regardless the outcome of the exams. You know that. Why don't you? You know he admires you.

Lee: Yes, I am grateful for that. Your father has been so good to me, I will never forget. But, I don't like friction; I don't want to take sides. It's not that I don't respect him, I love him. I just want to stay clear of conflicts. Other people don't understand me; that's okay. But you should know that I would never betray him or you. Trust me. You must have faith in me.

Nien: Yes, of course I trust you and have faith in you. I have always admired you and respect you. Come on, it's getting late, you get some sleep. We'll talk about it some other time. (Yells out loud toward the back room) Ching-yu, I am leaving. (Ching-yu comes out sees Nien off and closes the door. Mother comes out too).

Mom: Ching-yu, you go to bed, let me wait up for your brothers and sisters.

Ching-yu: Thanks Mom, good night. (Exits stage to back room).

Mom: Shang-Yin, are you feeling any better now?

Lee: Mom, I wasn't drunk. I wasn't feeling bad either.

Mom: Good, I want to discuss something important with you. Just before you came home, General Lee was here to see us. He came to offer a match for your marriage.

Lee: Mom, my heart already belongs to somebody else. I don't need any matchmaker.

Mom: How can you talk like that, especially when they are so good to you? Do you know who he had in mind for you?

Lee: (A bit nervously) Who?

Mom: The second daughter of Governor Wong. Her older sister is married to Master Han; don't you remember? You were at the wedding. If you marry her, you and Master Han will be in-laws. Wouldn't that be wonderful?

Lee: No Mom, just think of that family's wealth and power and then take a look at us. Forget it; it wouldn't be a good match.

Mom: I know that. I told the General that too. He said that the Governor doesn't care about money or power, he has them all. He is searching for quality, and he likes you because your intellectual abilities.

Lee: Mom, no, I don't want this marriage. Please turn them down. Tell them that I appreciate their thoughts, but I really can't accept.

Mom: Won't you even give it some time and think about it?

Lee: (Painfully) Mom, I have all the love that I want; there is no room for anyone else.

Mom: You... you still can't forget that Princess?

Lee: (Getting upset and excited) Mom, I am sorry I can't listen to you... I love her. Since the first time we were together I have vowed that I will love her forever, until death does us part. (kneeling near Mom) Mom, I am sorry for disobeying you. I would rather die than live without her. Forgive me for risking our lives. Please don't make me betray my vow. (sobbing).

Mom: All right! Stop this, you get up.

Lee: I am not getting up unless you promise me that you are not going to force me.

Mom: (sighing) Ai! Shang-Yin, this is a marriage made in heaven, and you want me to turn it down. Why are you so stubborn? Why are you making it so hard on yourself? Watching you carry on like this, it's killing me. (She begins to sob too.).

48

Lee: Mom...

Mom: Son, we have been through this before. You are no longer a child; you should know the consequences. To risk your life and our family name for a concubine, I... I don't even know what to say.

Lee: (Getting up) All right, Mom. I won't force you to agree with me, but please don't force this marriage on me either. Phoenix entrusts her love to me. I can't betray her to marry someone else.

Mom: Shang-Yin, General Lee is your friend, he has been so good to you. He chooses you because he respects you. What are you going to say to him?

Lee: (Loudly) I don't know, Mom, I don't have an answer. I am tormented enough; please leave me alone.

Mom: (Sadly) Yes, my dear. Give yourself some time to think it over. I am tired and I am going to bed. (Turns around and walks toward the back room, talking to herself, then off stage) AI, I know you are hurting. It hurts me more inside.

Lee: (sits down, thinking. He stares at the candle for a moment or so, then sighs and comes up with a few lines of a new poem) Ai! You, poor candle. You are more pathetic than I am. You are dripping tears. When will you stop?[7]

(The silk-worms of spring will weave until they die. And every night the candles will weep their wicks away.)[8] My love to you is just like... (Someone knocks lightly on the door, startling Lee) Somebody at the door? (He walks toward the door) Who is it?

Merry: Is Master Lee home?

Lee: Who are you? What do you want?

Merry: It's me, Merry.

[7] Three Hundred Poems of the Tang Dynasty 618-906. An English Translation v. Chinese Text. Witter Bynner. Tung Hai Book Co., Taichung, Taiwan, 1967.

[8] as translated by Elizabeth Moxon.

49

Lee: (Opens the door, happily greets Merry who wears commoner's clothing) Merry, did the Princess send you?

Merry: (Nods and takes a letter out of his pocket, hands it to Lee. While Lee reads the letter, Merry continues) Yes, her Highness wanted me to bring this letter to you. She misses you. She is back at the resort palace, and she wants to see you.

Lee: (Reads the letter, nodding and smiling at the same time) Yes... Yes... I'll go. I can't wait to see her. Merry, thank you.

Merry: You are most welcome. I better go before they find me missing. You be careful, and I'll see you soon. (Hurries off the stage. Lee closes the door and Mother comes out from the back room).

Mom: Who was it?

Lee: (Trying to cover up) Nobody. What are you talking about?

Mom: Oh? I thought I heard you talking to someone.

Lee: Oh, that. It was somebody who was lost and asking me for directions.

Mom: Oh! It's late; you better go to bed now, we've got a long day tomorrow.

Lights out, the end of Act 3.

Act 4

Time: Two years later. Winter.

Scenery: Winter vacation resort Palace interior. It is not as formal as the main Palace, but still with all the opulence.

Characters: Phoenix, Argus, Jade, Merry, Lee, Princess Young, Ien, Palace guards.

Curtain rises and lights rise. You can also hear the north winter wind whistling in the background. The atmosphere is cold and lonely. Phoenix is sitting alone, playing the harp. Backstage, a female vocalist is singing in a sad tone, as the background music, "Time was long before I met her, but is longer since we parted. And the east winds arisen and a hundred flowers are gone. And the silkworms of spring will weave until they die. And every night the candles will weep their wicks away. "[9]

(Our meetings are hard and our partings are even harder. The East wind had died down, ruined hundreds of blossoms. The silk worms weave silk until they die. The candles shed their tears until they burn out. [10] (Suddenly one of the harp's string breaks; the singing stops too).

Jade: (Cames out from back, with a cape in hand) Your Highness, you'd better put the cape on. It is raw and it looks like it's going to snow soon. You don't want to catch a chill.

Phoenix: The string broke. It may be a bad omen. I hope Shang-Yin didn't change his mind, and is not coming. No, he always comes. Lately though, I feel restless and uneasy. I hope nothing bad is going to happen. I am scared. (Outside, there are noises, Jade goes out to check and comes right back in).

[9] Three Hundred Poems of the Tang Dynasty 618-906. An English Translation v. Chinese Text. Witter Bynner. Tung Hai Book Co., Taichung, Taiwan, 1967.

[10] as translated by Elizabeth Moxon.

51

Jade: Your Highness, Princess Argus is here to see you. (Argus follows Jade in).

Argus: Are you feeling better? Did you take the medicine that I sent you? Did it work?

Phoenix: Calm down dear sister. Yes, thank you. I am much better.

Argus: Phoenix, I have some news for you. I overheard a rumor that the Crown Prince committed suicide, but that was just a coverup. The Crown prince was only twelve, too young to be depressed enough to commit suicide. In reality, people think he was murdered, and then it was made to look like he hanged himself.

Phoenix: That sounds logical. Granted, The Crown Prince did play around quite a bit much with those dancers and musicians. His extroverted personality made him want to be with those people to have fun. A child with that kind of personality; it's unlikely that he would be depressed enough to kill himself. Even though the Emperor punished those who taught him bad things.

Argus: That is what they all say. It must have something to do with that snake Princess Young. Do you remember four years ago when the would be "Queen" Princess Wong died mysteriously too? Afterwards, the snake woman constantly criticized Princess Wong's son, the Crown Prince, in front of the Emperor. She accused the Crown Prince of being too playful to be a good future Emperor. She wanted the Emperor to change heirs, to crown someone else for the throne. It was only after the most senior officials' opposition, that the whole thing was stopped. Now the Crown Prince is dead.

Phoenix: (continues for Argus) It created a chance that the Emperor might crown Princess Young's adopted son to be the future Emperor.

Argus: You are right, she is too smart to do it herself. But she does have spies and accomplices all over the Palace. Phoenix, you better be careful. You have produced a son for the Emperor. You also pose a possible obstacle to her plan. You could be next.

Phoenix: (Frightened) Oh, no. My son has no interest in the throne. And I don't want to be the "Queen". Don't scare me please.

Argus: Although you won't hurt others, you must prevent others from hurting you. In your situation now, you better use your head and

end this mad passion. This affair will get you all killed, if she ever gets any evidence.

Phoenix: You want me to part with him? I... I can't... I love him; I can't live without him.

Argus: You can't live without him? What about your son's life? Do you want him to live or not? The way you two carry on, sooner or later... Do you really think that with the snake woman staying with the Emperor in the Capital, that you will be safe here? You are wrong. You are dreaming. She has people watching you every minute. She knows every move you make. When the time comes, she'll catch you in action. She'll put you all to death.

Phoenix: (Frightened, starts to cry) Oh, no, you are scaring me. She wouldn't do that. She knows that I don't want her Emperor. She can keep him all to herself. Just leave me alone.

Argus: Don't cry. I didn't mean to frighten you. I am your blood sister, I love you, that's why I am telling you all this. I just want to warn you, so that you won't be alarmed and you will be prepared.
All right, let's change to a different subject. You are sweet and kind, but too naive. Let me ask you, do you know that the power struggle has divided our imperial officials into two groups?

Phoenix: Yes, I heard that had happened.

Argus: Did you know that your lover boy worked for Governor Nien until the Governor died? Now he's switched to the opposite party and works for Governor Wong. People say that he has no integrity, no loyalty. How can you love or trust a person like that. He probably is cheating you and using you too.

Phoenix: Oh, no, you are wrong. People misjudged Shang-Yin, he is not like that. He told me that he worked for Governor Nien from the time that he was very young, because they were poor and the Niens had been good to his family. Governor Wong and General Lee treated him as an equal and with respect. Out of gratitude, he worked for them. He is not interested in political power or money. The fact is that he despises conflict. All he wants is to be neutral, to accomplish things without getting involved in either party. I admire him, I regard him as superior and above all others.

Argus: Is he? How can you be so sure, Phoenix? I just heard some news. It will break your heart, but I have to tell you, so you can make up your mind what to do with your life.

Phoenix: What is it? Tell me.

Argus: Somebody told me that Shang-Yin is getting married, and his future wife is the second daughter of Governor Wong.

Phoenix: (Shocked) He's... getting...married? (heart broken, she starts to cry).

Argus: People have said that that is why he suddenly took a high ranking office.

Phoenix: He told me that now he has finally gotten what he deserved for his years of hard work. Did he lie to me? No... no, I don't believe it; he is not like that.

Argus: Sis... this love has blinded you. Calm down... wipe your tears... forget about him. From now on you are finished with him, you hear me?

Phoenix: No...no.... Sister. I can't finish with him. Jade, please go outside to check. When Shang-Yin arrives, come in and tell me first.

Jade: Yes, your Highness. (Jade goes off stage).

Phoenix: (Making sure that no one is around) Sis... I can't leave him now; to tell you the truth, I am with his child.

Argus: What? You are expecting his child? Are you crazy? Are you sure it's his?

Phoenix: Don't be silly. The Emperor hasn't been here for a long time. I only love him. There has been no one else.

Argus: No wonder you haven't felt well lately.

Phoenix: What should I do?

Argus: How far along are you?

Phoenix: A little short of three months.

Argus: (Looks at Phoenix's belly closely) It doesn't show yet, but sooner or later people will notice.

Phoenix: I thought about going back to the palace, and working on the Emperor. Maybe he will have me for one night. That way I can keep the baby.

Argus: Don't be silly, it won't work that way. It will only raise the Emperor's suspicion. Even if you succeed and He spends time with you, that snake woman will have you put to death. The safest way out is to get rid of it. Take medication and abort it. No one will know.

Phoenix: No, I can't. This is our own flesh and blood, the product of our love.

Argus: Wake up dear sister. I am afraid that you have no choice. If you don't get rid of it, no one can save you.

Jade: (Comes in announcing Lee's arrival) Your Highness, Master Lee is here.

Argus: You and Jade go inside for a while. Let me talk to him first, see what he has to say.

Jade: Come on, let's get some rest first. (Both exit off stage. Lee comes on stage in a palace worker's clothing).

Lee: How are you Princess Argus. It's nice to see you here. Where is Phoenix?

Argus: She is inside. I came over to see her because she didn't feel well. She just finished throwing up and is lying down now. I have sent for the royal physicians; they should be here soon.

Lee: Oh? I hope it's nothing serious. Do you think it's a cold or something she ate.

Argus: I think it's... Jade, please go outside and look out for me. If you see someone coming, signal me.

Jade: Yes, your Highness. (Jade exits off stage).

Argus: By the way, before I forget, I must congratulate you on your appointment to new position.

Lee: Dear Princess, please don't embarrass me. Passing the test was long overdue. I had such bad luck with it, and the new post is hardly worth mentioning.

Argus: Well, it's much better than before. I heard that Governor Wong admired your talents and asked you to handle important documents between him and the Emperor. The Governor also likes you enough that he wants you to marry his second daughter, to be his son in law. Are these things all true?

Lee: Dear Sis, please don't sound so cold and distant. What you have heard is all true, except I love your sister more than anything. Even though The Governor has the marriage in mind, I have dragged my feet on answering the match makers, I love only Phoenix.

Argus: You sound very sincere. If you do truly love my sister, what are you going to do about it?

Lee: That is the question I have thought about for a long time and can't figure a good answer.

Argus: You two have been together for four years now. I believe you are an honest man and truly love her. Each time you see each other, you put your lives on the line. Now she is pregnant, and, if you don't do something about it, you all will die.

Lee: (Shocked yet happy) She is? She is with my child? Our child?

Argus: Don't be so happy. The Emperor has not been here for a long time. If she is pregnant, it means death for her. Even you can't get away with that.

Lee: (Changes to a concerned look) What can we do?

Argus: Phoenix doesn't know what to do either.....You cause the problem, you deal with it......

Lee: Yes, dear sister, I know it's all my fault. I take full responsibility, but tell me what to do.

Argus: What responsibility? You can't tell the Emperor that it's your fault, so you'll marry her and make a honest woman out of her. You can't ask the Emperor to spare her and punish only you. You have only one choice.

Lee: Tell me, I'll do anything for her.

Argus: I've got an idea, but Phoenix doesn't like it.

Lee: What is it? I'll do it.

Argus: It has nothing to do with you. I want her to take some medicine to abort the baby, but she won't go along with it.

Lee: I... I don't like it either. It's our flesh and blood, the creation of our love and passion. I can't destroy a new life.

Argus: Destroy a new life? If the Emperor finds out, he will destroy all your lives. Then what?

Lee: I don't care; I love Phoenix. I will do whatever she wants me to. If we can't live together, I would rather die together. Life would be meaningless without her.

Argus: (visibly moved) You really love her, don't you?

Lee: (Firmly) More than anything in this world.

Phoenix: (Rushing out from inside) Shan-Yin... I love you too. I hope God will take pity on our love and give us a chance to live.

Lee: Let's give this some serious thought, to see if we can figure something out.

Argus: Other than my suggestion, I can't think of anything that is safe.

Lee:(Thinking while Argus was talking) Maybe there is a way out.

Phoenix: What is it?

Lee: When I was young, I once lived in a Taoist temple. Maybe I can find a temple for nuns and ask them to take you in. Then, you go to the Emperor to request permission to become a nun. After you get away from the Palace, stay in the temple for a while until we are safe. Then we can plan for the future.

Phoenix: Yes, you are brilliant. This is great; the only problem is, will the Emperor let me go?

Argus: You have not been the Emperor's favorite for a long time. As long as you are persistent, he just might let you offer yourself to God. The Emperor would love to have people pray for him constantly.

Lee: Let's give it a try. What do we have to lose. We must keep our plan secret though.

Argus: Yes, if anything goes wrong, we'll be finished. From now on, you'd better not come here any more, to avoid any risk.

Lee: Phoenix, Sis is right. We will not see each other for a while for the benefit of our future.

Phoenix: I guess so. I'll miss you, and I'll pray for us, my love.

Lee: (Suddenly remembers, takes a jade plate out of his pocket) Oh! With all the excitement, I almost forgot about this. I had this made specially for you. This is a poem I wrote for you and had a craftsman carve on this jade plate to symbolize our love.

Phoenix: (accepts the plate, and reads the poem on the plate) "Now that candle-shadow stands on the screen of carved marble. And the River of Heaven slants and the morning stars are low, Are you sorry for having stolen the potion that has sent you over purple seas and blue skies, to brood through the long nights?" [11]

(The flickering candle casts deep shadows against the marble screen. The milky way is fading and the morning stars diminish. The moon goddess in solitude regrets having stolen the magic potion. Over blue seas and clear skies, now to brood through long lonely nights.)[12]

Phoenix: Shang-Yin. How did you come up with this?

Lee: Don't you remember? A short while ago, on the moon festival, we walked along the Chu-Jiang riverbank. Under the bright moon light I pointed out, there was one moon up in the sky and one in the water. The two were staring at each other like lovers, how romantic. You naughty thing; you picked up a pebble and deliberately threw it in the water and broke the moon in the water. To symbolize our love like the fullest moon which will never break in our hearts, I give you this Jade plate.

[11] ibid. Witter Bynner.
[12] ibid. Elizabeth Moxon.

Phoenix: Thank you; I love your poetic thoughts and romantic feelings. I'll forever treasure this. When I see the plate, it's as if I am seeing you with me. (Puts the plate on the table, and holds Shang-Yin).

(Jade hurries in, followed by Merry).

Jade: Your highness, we have trouble. Merry is here to warn us.

Merry: Your Highness, I saw Princess Young leading a group of guards coming in this direction. She said that they were searching for the killer of the Crown Prince. (Turns to Lee) I think they are aiming for you. You better do something. Take care of yourself. I have to go, I can't let her see me here. (Finishes and hurries off stage).

Phoenix: What! She is coming toward here?

Argus: I told you. She is not going to leave you alone. Shang-Yin, you better run, if they see you, we'll all be dead.

Phoenix: Jade, lead him through the secret passage. Be careful... hurry... go... go... farewell my love.

Jade: Yes, I know, come along. Hurry. (Drags Lee off stage while he continues to talk and Phoenix tries to hold him again).

Lee: I'll work on our plan; I'll see you soon. I love you. Please be careful, my love.

Argus: (Looks around and tries to clean up, puts the plate in a drawer) Phoenix, pull yourself together. You must handle her with caution. Be careful what you say. You better burn those letters and poems he wrote you. If they find them, you'll be in deep trouble.

Phoenix: Yes, Argus, I am doing it now. (Outside, there are soldiers' footsteps. Ien's voice is giving out orders).

Ien: All guards to attention. Surround this part of the Palace. No one is allowed to trespass. Any one who looks suspicious, bring to me; take no chances, is that clear?

(All the soldiers say yes in unison. Then the footsteps spread out. Ien shows up on stage at the main entrance).

Ien: Her highness Princess Young is here.

(Phoenix and Argus walk toward the entrance, kneel down in greeting, while Young walks onto the stage).

Argus: Welcome, Your Highness.

Phoenix: Welcome Your Highness.

Young: At ease. (sits down)

Phoenix: Your Highness, it is a bitter cold day; you have come all the way from the Imperial Palace to here. Your Highness must have important orders for me. I am at your service.

Young: (sounding very phony) Oh!... nothing really that important. Our Emperor has sent me to make the rounds, doing inspections. Apparently, there are rumors that some low level female servants are not obeying the Palace rules and regulations. The Emperor wants me to straighten things out. I am here just to do my job. If my presence offends you, please forgive me.

Phoenix: I have strict orders here for my people to follow the rules. Plus the guards are all over the place. How could anyone have a chance to do anything improper?

Young: I know that you are strict, but you can't be careful enough. (Her face changes from a smile to a snarl.) Guards, check the rooms. I want a thorough search. (The guards come on stage and listen to Young) Look for things that belong to men. If you find any, bring them to me immediately.

Guards: Yes. (They start searching the back rooms).

(Phoenix is nervous. Argus sees this and tries to say something to help).

Argus: Your Highness, how could anybody start such a poisonous rumor and cause such a disturbance. You see, it makes you upset, which is not good for your health. It also takes you away from the fun things that you and our Emperor might be doing.

Young: You are so right; the rumors are terrible. Ever since the Crown Prince died, all kinds of nasty rumors have been aimed at me. Fortunately, our Emperor trusts me. Otherwise, I would have been sent to the isolation chamber to die there.

(The guards come back and their leader reports to Young).

Guard: Your Highness, we could not find anything that looks suspicious.

Ien: Your Highness, it is snowing outside.

Young: Oh!... yes... good. Now you go outside, tell the rest of them to check the garden and path, follow any footprints in the snow that you see. The rest of you continue searching here.

Guards: Yes, Your Highness.

(One goes off stage through the main entrance; the rest start looking on stage. One guard opens a drawer and takes out the plate, looks at it and hands to Young).

Young: (Smiles cruelly) What is this? Is it from our Emperor?

Phoenix: (Nervously) Your Highness... It's from my... father.

Young: Your father? Argus, you are older. Do you have one?

Argus: (Alertly) Yes Your highness. I had one too, but I broke mine, a long time ago.

Young: (Looks at the poem and reads a little to herself) Phoenix, Did your father write this poem?

Phoenix: No, I... I wrote it.

Young: I can't believe that you can write this well. Ien, I am getting cold, take me back to the Palace. I am taking this jade plate with me. I'll give to the Emperor and let him figure it out. (Gets up).

Ien: Yes, Your Highness. (Helps her with the cape, and leads the way, out the main entrance).

(After a moment of silence on stage).

Phoenix: Argus, what are we going to do?

Argus: (Holds Phoenix in her arms, bravely) Come, come. Whatever will be, will be. Don't worry, you have me, I love you.

61

(Outside, the wind blows, snowflakes fly and the lights gradually dim to dark).

END OF ACT FOUR

ACT FIVE

Time: Continues from Prelude. Nineteen years later. Winter.

Scenery: Same as Prelude. Lee's house. It is still snowing outside, almost the same as Act Four.

Characters: Lee is forty seven years old with white hair and in poor health. Han has aged nicely, he is in better spirits. Ching-yu is in his thirties. Argus, Phoenix and Jade look the same due to their appearances as ghosts.

When the curtain goes up, It returns back to the Prelude. Lee and Han are sitting opposite each other, talking and drinking.

Lee: Ai... Let's drink to the past.

Han: Gladly, my friend. (Both drain their glasses. Han pours more for Shang-yin).

Han: Yee-san. When young people are in love, often they make mistakes, but most are unintentional. It is forgivable; you shouldn't be too hard on yourself.

Lee: (Staring into space and reciting) And a moment that ought to have lasted for ever, has come and gone before I knew... (The music of the main theme starts. Lee takes the harp off the wall, plays a few notes then stops. Continually drowned to the past in pain).

Han: Yee-san, what's wrong?

(No response from Lee.)

Han: Hey, Yee-san, come on, continue your story. What happened then?

Lee: (coming back to reality) Oh! Where was I?

Han: You were saying that the Princess Young brought Palace guards there searching for you. Jade led you out to safety, through the secret passage.

63

Lee: Oh, yes, I still remember clearly, that day was bitter cold with a north wind howling. It was just starting to snow. Frankly, I was lucky to get out alive. I couldn't sleep or eat for days. I was worrying about Phoenix. I wondered what they would do to her.

Han: They might have tortured her in order to get a confession.

Lee: I wanted to save her or at least find out some information. Who could I ask? I didn't even know where or how to start. I paced along the river bank like the ants on a hot pot. Can you imagine, I couldn't do a darn thing to help her.

Han: Then, what happened?

Lee: Three days later, she sent a messenger to bring me a letter and her Inlaid Harp. (Lee strokes the harp gently as if he were touching her) She taught me how to play. This is the only thing left between us.

Han: What did her letter say?

Lee: She... (Lee starts to cry).

Han: When did she write the letter?

Lee: She wrote the letter before they got her.

Han: Then, what happened?

Lee: Then? That was the end of her.

Han: Did the Emperor give her a death wish?

Lee: No, She didn't want to drag me down. She jumped into the well before they could do anything.

Han: My God, she killed herself to spare you?

Lee: Yes, she did... to save me. The letter was to tell me that she didn't want to risk mentioning my name if she was tortured. She killed herself before they even arrested her. The messenger also told me that, shortly after she died, her sister Argus also jumped into the same well. From that day on I lost any happiness in life.

Han: (Wipes his own tears) Oh dear! Finally, after all these years, I just understand now, why you never smiled on your wedding day. Do you remember? I kept asking you what was wrong, and you wouldn't answer me. Now that I know what you went through, oh, I am so sorry.

Lee: It was the saddest time of my whole entire life. My heart was broken into pieces. This is a secret that I have never told any one. (Laughs sadly and shakes his head) After a few drinks, I reveal my soul to you... my friend.

Han: Don't worry, I will never tell anyone. I promise, I won't even tell my wife.

Lee: Yes, please. Bless my wife's soul, I hope her spirit will understand and forgive me.

Han: (Takes a look at the outside sky; it's dark and windy) I better go. You are not well and look tired, Get some rest.

Lee: (looking a little drunk) No, I am fine. When you drink with good friends, you never have enough. Don't go. Keep me company.....

Han: No, for your sake, I must go. We'll drink some other time. Good bye. (Han leaves. Lee reluctantly sees him off. Then Lee comes back and drinks some more).

Lee: (Talking to himself) Cheers. (Pours himself another one) Only when I have enough, then, I can stop thinking.

(Lights gradually dim).

(When the lights brighten again, a double of Lee is sleeping on the table, snoring. Lee is standing behind his double in order to show that he is dreaming)

(Some one knocks on the door; Lee goes to open the door).

Lee: Who is it?

Phoenix: It is me... Phoenix.

Lee: (Surprised but happy) Who? Did you say Phoenix? (Lee opens the door. Phoenix comes on stage in the midst of smoke created by dry ice).

Lee: (Grasps Phoenix and keeps checking) Is this really you?

Phoenix: Of course dear, it's me. Have you forgotten about me?

Lee: (Holds on to her and cries) No, no, Of course not. I miss you so
    much. I pray every day to see you again. Finally you are here. I can
    hold you now.

Phoenix: My love, I am here for you. (holding him tight for a while then
    looking at him) You have changed so much, my love... (He starts to
    cry again)
I am so sorry that you are in such pain. (She holds him again, after a while,
    they separate and look at each other).

Lee: It has been almost twenty years. Let me look at you. You have not
    changed at all. Did you miss me?

Phoenix: Of course I missed you. I have not let one minute go by without
    thinking about you.

Lee: I must be in a dream. How come, after all these years, I get to see you
    again?

Phoenix: Life is a dream. Do you remember, those days, we were so
    happy when we were together? Didn't it feel like a happy dream to
    you? Your ups and downs in career and life, didn't it feel like a
    nightmare? Who can say what is a dream and what is not?

Lee: Yes, you are so right. As long as I can be with you, I don't care.

Phoenix: I know. Since your wife passed away, you have been alone.
    You refuse to have any one to look after you. You even turned
    your superior down, when he offered you a woman to serve and
    accompany you. Why are you so hard on yourself? It hurts me to
    see you suffer like this. It breaks my heart to see you sick and
    lonely. Especially on a snowy winter night. (She cries out loud).

Lee: (Holds her and comforts her) Come on. Now that you are here,
    everything will be fine. Don't mention snowy winter nights. It was
    that snowy winter night, when we were separated. Since then,
    every snowy winter night, I have thought about you. It makes my
    heart ache, and breaks my spirit into pieces.

Phoenix: (Looks at the harp) My love, the harp... you still have it; do you play it often?

Lee: No. When I see it, it... it reminds me of you. It hurts too much. I used to afraid and worry about too many things. Now that's all behind us. Guess what, we even outlive a few Emperors. You are free now. We can be together; no one is in our way. Nothing can stop us now. We finally can live happily ever after. (Holds her tightly again).

Phoenix: Oh, my love, you still love me? You didn't forget?

Lee: No, of course not, you silly thing. I will always love you forever and ever. (holds her even tighter. Suddenly Jade appears too).

Jade: Your Highness. You have stayed too long. Come on, let's go, hurry.

Phoenix: No, I am not leaving. I'll never leave him again.

Lee: Phoenix. Don't go Don't leave me. (Jade pulls Phoenix. Lee pulls her too, and while they are struggling, Argus appears on stage too).

Argus: Phoenix, come on, it's time to leave. We must go. If you delay any further, we will all be in trouble.

Phoenix: Why must I go? I want to be with him.

Argus: (Slowly and emotionlessly) He is coming to join us soon. You'll see, pretty soon you two are going to be together forever.

(Argus and Jade pull Phoenix away and off stage into the dark. Lee goes after them and calls out for Phoenix. Lights dim).
(A rooster crows in the distance. Gradually day light breaks, and the stage brightens again. Lee wakes up from the table, rubs his eyes, and talks to the sky).

Lee: Phoenix, wait for me. I am coming to join you... soon.

The lights go out and the curtain falls.

THE END

Translator's Note:

The author, Mr. Chiang asked me to translate this play in 1993. I hesitated to take on the job, for many reasons. This is a classical play, like the Shakespearean plays of the western world. For my humble literary background, it's out of my league. While I was reading the play, I saw many of the difficulties and obstacles that would occur during the translation. Besides, who in the western world would want to see or read a story about an old Chinese poet anyway. A computer illiterate like myself with this kind of translation task, means a difficult editing job for John.

So, I kept putting it off, and kept feeling guilty. After all, Lee-Shang-Yin is my favorite poet, and, if I didn't do the translation to make it available, there would be no chance for any westerner to know any thing about him. So, with John's urging and one of the Buddha's sayings, "If I don't go to Hell to save sinners, who will?", I started to read and study the play.

Then, in the spring of 1994, the author told me that he wanted to rewrite Act one while I was working on the rest of the play. I finished most of the draft in March, 1994. Meanwhile, the author retired from China Television Co., and was busy with other things. I found myself a job, and that was the end of work on the play for a year.

In April, 1995, I had major surgery, coming home on Easter Sunday. That evening, one of my daughters, Alma, lost a classmate in a car accident. It reminded me again how fragile life can be. There were so many things I had not accomplished or completed, and the play was one of them. I wrote to Mr. Chiang, and he had just finished the new version of Act One.

In May, I went back into the hospital for back surgery. During the time I was home on temporary disability, there wasn't much I could do but rest. While I was lying down, I would ponder the translation. Then I would sit up and type on the computer again until the pain started.

With most of the characters in the play I have used the sound of their names, such as Lee, Han...etc. With others I have used their roles, such as mother, soldier, guard; for the most part, they are self explanatory. In the cases of Princess Phoenix and Argus, I used the meanings of their names because of the beauty of these mythical Chinese birds. It would be less enjoyable for Westerners to read this play if I had translated in the strict Chinese conversational style. At times, I tried to make them sound close to the western classical such as "Knights Of The Round Table", "Ivanhoe", "Robin hood"....etc., so that the reader can find some familiarity.

The most difficult part for me to translate was "The Poems". I am not well qualified to translate his work. The only reference book available in English to me was <u>Three Hundred Poems of The T'Ang Dynasty</u>, by Witter Bynner. Although all of the poems in the play are well known, I worked more carefully on their translation to convey more feelings. I list Mr. Bynner's translation first, followed by my version. I did so for two reasons. I quoted Mr. Bynner's translation so that the reader has the version of an American poet's version of Chinese poetry. Secondly, although my translations of poetry are not necessarily that good, at least I am diligent enough to do it and not just quote Mr. Bynner's work.

One major element that has kept the author and myself working nicely together has been his trust in me. He gave me full consent to do whatever necessary to make the play enjoyable to the reader. Again I thank John Moxon for his encouragement, editing, and polishing my English to make this project possible.